delicious noodles

The Confident Cooking Promise of Success

Welcome to the world of Confident Cooking,
where recipes are double-tested by our team
of home economists to achieve a high standard
of success—and delicious results every time.

bay books

TEST KITCHEN PERFECTION

You'll never make a wrong move with a step-by-step cookbook. Our team of home economists has tested and refined the recipes so that you can create fabulous food in your own kitchen. Follow our easy instructions and step-by-step photographs and you'll feel like there is a master chef in the kitchen guiding you every step of the way.

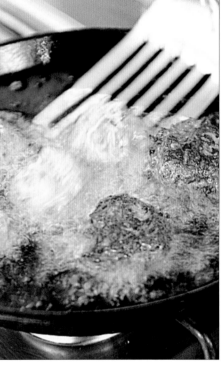

All recipes are double-tested by our team of home economists. When we test our recipes, we rate them for ease of preparation. The following cookery ratings are on the recipes in this book, making them easy to use and understand.

A single Cooking with Confidence symbol indicates a recipe that is simple and generally quick to make—perfect for beginners.

Two symbols indicate the need for just a little more care and a little more time.

Three symbols indicate special dishes that need more investment in time, care and patience—but the results are worth it.

IMPORTANT

Those who might be at risk from the effects of salmonella food poisoning (the elderly, pregnant women, young children and those suffering from immune deficiency diseases) should consult their doctor with any concerns about eating raw eggs.

The Publisher thanks: AEG Kitchen Appliances, Liebherr Refrigeration and Wine Cellars; Artiques & Country; Bay Swiss; Bertolli Olive Oil; Breville Holdings Pty Ltd; Chief Australia; Global Treasures; Kitchen Aid; Les Olivades; No Chintz; Pacific East India Company; Papaya Studio; Sheldon & Hammond; Tree of Life.

FRONT COVER: *Crab and papaya noodle salad* PAGE 44.
INSIDE FRONT COVER: *Singapore noodles* PAGE 76.
BACK COVER: *Chilli salt squid and cellophane noodle salad* PAGE 50.

CONTENTS

ABOVE: *Pork and prawn vermicelli* PAGE 97.
TOP RIGHT: *Somen noodles* PAGE 5.
RIGHT: *Buddhist vegetarian noodles* PAGE 85.

WHAT NOODLE IS THIS?

EGG NOODLES

Are made of wheat flour and eggs, and are widely available both fresh and dried. The thin round variety are used in soups, stir-fries and for deep-frying, while the flatter, wider noodles are used mainly in soups. Fresh egg noodles will store refrigerated for up to a week. Cook in boiling water for 1 minute, then drain, rinse and add to the dish. Dried noodles will keep indefinitely—cook for 3 minutes until tender, then rinse and drain. If using in soups, they can be added straight to the pan.

HOKKIEN EGG NOODLES

Originally Chinese, these noodles are a staple of Malaysian noodle dishes. They are a thick, fresh egg noodle, which has been cooked and lightly oiled before packaging. They only need to be covered with boiling water for 1 minute to separate, before being drained and rinsed. Their strength and thickness makes them perfect for stir-frying, as they absorb the flavour of the sauce—they are also used in soups and noodle salads.

MUNG BEAN VERMICELLI
(CELLOPHANE OR GLASS NOODLES)

Are made with a mixture of mung bean and tapioca starches, and water. They are sold dried in tight opaque bundles. They are difficult to cut or separate, so try to buy in smaller bundles or cut with scissors. They can be deep-fried straight from the packet, eaten as a soft noodle, and are ideal for soups and hotpots. Soak in boiling water for 3–4 minutes, then rinse and drain. They have a soft gelatinous texture, and become almost transparent.

RICE STICK NOODLES

Are available dried and may be a little thicker than rice vermicelli, or a flat medium-width noodle. Soak in warm water for 15–20 minutes until al dente. Drain and add to stir-fries. For soups, cook in boiling water for 5 minutes.

DRIED RICE VERMICELLI

Are thread-like white noodles made with rice flour, used in soups, stir-fries and spring rolls. Deep-fry straight from the packet, until puffed and crispy. Or, soak in boiling water for 6–7 minutes, drain and rinse to use as a soft noodle.

SHANGHAI NOODLES

These thick, round egg noodles are similar to Hokkien noodles but are not cooked, or oiled. They are sold fresh and will keep refrigerated for up to 4 days. Before using, cook the noodles in boiling water for 4–5 minutes, then drain and rinse. Use these noodles as an alternative to Hokkien noodles, particularly in dishes where the sauce tends to be oily, or in traditional Shanghai noodle dishes.

SOBA NOODLES

Are Japanese noodles made from buckwheat flour, or a combination of buckwheat and wheat flour. They are available fresh, though more easily found dried. Usually eaten in a simple broth, or served cold with a dipping sauce. Add the noodles to a large saucepan of boiling water and stir to separate. Return to the boil, adding 1 cup (250 ml) cold water and repeat this step 3 times, as it comes to the boil. Drain and rinse under cold water until cold.

POTATO STARCH NOODLES
(KOREAN VERMICELLI)
Are made from sweet potato starch and are available dried in bundles. They are chewy in texture and are used in soups and stir-fries, where they soak up the sauce. Before use, soak in boiling water for 10 minutes until softened, or cook in boiling water for 3 minutes, then drain and rinse. They will become plump and gelatinous when cooked, but take care as they can become gluggy and begin to break down.

RAMEN NOODLES
Originated in China, but are now more popular all over Japan. Ramen are a wheat noodle bound together with egg and are available fresh, dried or instant. They need to be boiled before use—2 minutes for fresh noodles, 4 minutes for dried, and for instant, just add boiling stock. Fresh ramen should be kept refrigerated for up to 4 days. They are traditionally served in a hot broth; the instant variety are a snack food enjoyed all over Japan.

RICE SHEET/RICE NOODLES
Are made with rice flour, then steamed and oiled before packaging. Best used as soon as possible after buying, as they will harden if refrigerated. Available as a fresh 'sheet' and cut to the desired width. Cover with boiling water and gently separate—a silky texture makes them ideal for stir-fries and soups. 'Sheets' can be filled, rolled and steamed. Pre-cut noodles are available, as long noodles (round or flat), in varying thicknesses. Cover with boiling water and gently separate. Drain and rinse.

SOMEN NOODLES
These thin, delicate Japanese noodles made from wheat flour are commonly available dried, and need to be cooked in boiling water for 2 minutes, before draining and rinsing. Somen are traditionally eaten cold with a dipping sauce, but may also be served in broth. Some varieties have added green tea powder, egg yolk, or plum with shiso oil, which create different coloured and flavoured noodles.

UDON NOODLES
Are thick, white Japanese noodles made from wheat flour. They are most often eaten in soups, but also in hotpots and braised dishes. They are available in either fresh, frozen, dried or instant varieties, and need to be cooked in boiling water for 1–2 minutes, or until tender, but *al dente*, before draining and rinsing. Store fresh udon noodles in the refrigerator for up to 4 days.

WHEAT NOODLES
These are thin, round noodles made simply with wheat flour and water. They are available both fresh and dried, but are more commonly sold dried. Fresh noodles will keep refrigerated for up to a week, and will need to be boiled for 2 minutes before draining, rinsing and using, whereas dried noodles will need 4 minutes cooking. Wheat noodles are fabulous for stir-frying as they are quite strong, and will absorb the delicious flavours of their sauce.

ASIAN INGREDIENTS

BLACK FUNGUS
(CLOUD EAR, WOOD FUNGUS,
TREE EAR, OR MOUSE EAR)
Black fungus has little flavour of its own, but is prized for its crunchy texture. It is most commonly available dried and must be soaked in warm water for 20 minutes (until it is soft and jelly-like) before use. It is also available fresh.

BROWN BEAN PASTE
A seasoning made from yellow or black fermented and salted soy beans, this paste has been used by Chinese cooks to flavour food for thousands of years. There are two forms available: whole beans in a thick sauce, and mashed beans (sold as crushed or yellow bean sauce).

CANDLENUTS
Are large, waxy nuts similar in size to macadamia nuts, but with a drier texture. Candlenuts cannot be eaten raw as they are slightly toxic. Candlenuts are roasted, then ground (or crushed) and used as a thickening agent in dishes such as curries and sauces. They can be purchased in Indian and Asian supermarkets. If not available, macadamia nuts can be used instead.

CHINESE SESAME PASTE
Is a light brown, rich, creamy paste made from ground, roasted white sesame seeds. It is different from Lebanese tahini, which is made from raw sesame seeds and cannot be used as a substitute. It is added to sauces for both hot and cold dishes.

DASHI GRANULES
Are made from dried kelp (kombu) and dried fish (bonito). Dashi is available as granules or powder and is dissolved in hot water to make the well-known Japanese dashi stock.

MIZUNA
Is a Japanese green with a mild peppery flavour. Young leaves are often used in salads or as a garnish, while older leaves are used in stir-fries.

CHINESE BLACK AND
RED VINEGAR
Are types of rice vinegar made from
fermented rice. Black vinegar is a
dark, pungent, slightly sweet vinegar,
usually made from glutinous rice and
is very popular in northern China. Red
vinegar is a clear, pale, red rice vinegar
mainly used as a dipping sauce.

CHINESE CELERY
The celery stalks are thin and hollow
and have a stronger taste and smell
than Western celery. It is used in stir-
fries and soups or blanched and used
in salads. Ensure the leaves are green
and the stems are firm. If not available,
use regular celery.

CHINESE RICE WINE
Is an amber-coloured fermented rice
wine, with a rich sweetish taste. If
not available, use dry sherry instead—
grape wines are not suitable
substitutes.

THAI BASIL
May also be called holy basil. It is
a member of the basil family, but
has smaller and darker leaves than
common basil. The leaves are attached
to a purple stem and have a sweet
anise flavour. It may be used in stir-
fries, soups, curries and salads.

VIETNAMESE MINT
(LAKSA LEAF OR CAMBODIAN MINT)
This trailing herb with narrow, pointed
and pungent-tasting leaves does not
actually belong to the mint family,
despite its common name. Its flavour
resembles coriander (cilantro), but is
slightly sharper. It is eaten raw in
salads, or added to laksas as a garnish.

WAKAME
A curly-leaf brown algae with a mild
vegetable taste and soft texture. Most
commonly used in soups, dried
wakame can be used (after soaking
in boiling water) in salads or as a
vegetable. Use sparingly—its volume
increases about 10 times. You can use
kombu or other seaweeds if necessary.

SOUPS

CHICKEN LAKSA

Preparation time: 30 minutes +
  10 minutes soaking
Cooking time: 35 minutes
Serves 4–6

1½ tablespoons coriander seeds
1 tablespoon cumin seeds
1 teaspoon ground turmeric
1 onion, roughly chopped
1 tablespoon roughly chopped ginger
3 cloves garlic, peeled
3 stems lemon grass (white part only),
  sliced
6 candlenuts or macadamia nuts
  (see Notes)
4–6 small fresh red chillies
2–3 teaspoons shrimp paste, roasted
  (see Notes)
1 litre (4 cups) chicken stock
60 ml (¼ cup) oil
400 g (14 oz) chicken thigh fillets, cut
  into 2 cm (¾ inch) pieces
750 ml (3 cups) coconut milk
4 fresh makrut (kaffir) lime leaves
2½ tablespoons lime juice
2 tablespoons fish sauce
2 tablespoons grated palm sugar
  or soft brown sugar
250 g (9 oz) dried rice vermicelli
90 g (3¼ oz) bean sprouts
4 fried tofu puffs, julienned
3 tablespoons roughly chopped fresh
  Vietnamese mint
20 g (⅔ cup) fresh coriander (cilantro)
  leaves
lime wedges, to serve

1 Roast the coriander and cumin
seeds in a dry saucepan or frying pan
over medium heat for 1–2 minutes,
or until fragrant, tossing the pan
constantly to prevent them burning.
Grind finely in a mortar and pestle or
a spice grinder.
2 Place all the spices, onion, ginger,
garlic, lemon grass, candlenuts,
chillies and shrimp paste in a food
processor or blender. Add about
125 ml (½ cup) of the stock and
blend to a fine paste.
3 Heat the oil in a wok or large
saucepan over low heat and gently
cook the paste for 3–5 minutes,
stirring constantly to prevent it
burning or sticking to the bottom.
Add the remaining stock and bring
to the boil over high heat. Reduce
the heat to medium and simmer for
15 minutes, or until reduced slightly.
Add the chicken and simmer for
4–5 minutes, or until cooked through.
4 Add the coconut milk, lime leaves,
lime juice, fish sauce and palm sugar
and simmer for 5 minutes over
medium–low heat. Do not bring to
the boil or cover with a lid, as the
coconut milk will split.
5 Meanwhile, place the vermicelli in
a heatproof bowl, cover with boiling
water and soak for 6–7 minutes, or
until softened. Drain and divide
among large serving bowls with the
bean sprouts. Ladle the hot soup over
the top and garnish with some tofu
strips, mint and coriander leaves.
Serve with a wedge of lime.

NUTRITION PER SERVE (6)
Fat 42.5 g; Protein 22 g; Carbohydrate
40 g; Dietary Fibre 5 g; Cholesterol 58 mg;
2620 kJ (625 Cal)

COOK'S FILE
Notes: Raw candlenuts are slightly toxic
so must be cooked before use.
To roast the shrimp paste, wrap the
paste in foil and place under a hot
grill (broiler) for 1 minute.

ROAST DUCK WITH SHIITAKE MUSHROOMS AND FLAT RICE NOODLE BROTH

Preparation time: 25 minutes +
25 minutes soaking
Cooking time: 10 minutes
Serves 4–6

3 dried shiitake mushrooms
1 Chinese roast duck (1.5 kg or 3 lb 5 oz)
500 ml (2 cups) chicken stock
2 tablespoons light soy sauce
1 tablespoon Chinese rice wine
2 teaspoons sugar
400 g (14 oz) fresh flat rice noodles
2 tablespoons oil
3 spring onions (scallions), thinly sliced
1 teaspoon finely chopped ginger
400 g (14 oz) bok choy (pak choi), trimmed and leaves separated
1/4 teaspoon sesame oil

1 Place the shiitake mushrooms in a heatproof bowl, cover with 250 ml (1 cup) boiling water and soak for 20 minutes. Drain, reserving the liquid and squeezing the excess liquid from the mushrooms. Discard the woody stems and thinly slice the caps.
2 Remove the skin and flesh from the roast duck. Discard the fat and carcass. Finely slice the duck meat and the skin (you should have about 400 g or 14 oz of duck meat).
3 Place the chicken stock, soy sauce, rice wine, sugar and the reserved mushroom liquid in a saucepan over medium heat. Bring to a simmer and cook for 5 minutes.
4 Meanwhile, place the rice noodles in a heatproof bowl, cover with boiling water and soak briefly. Gently separate the noodles with your hands and drain well. Divide evenly among large soup bowls.
5 Heat the oil in a wok over high heat. Add the spring onion, ginger and shiitake mushrooms and cook for several seconds. Transfer to the broth with the bok choy and duck meat and simmer for 1 minute, or until the duck has warmed through and the bok choy has wilted. Ladle the soup on the noodles and drizzle sesame oil on each serving. Serve immediately.

NUTRITION PER SERVE (6)
Fat 23.5 g; Protein 17 g; Carbohydrate 31 g; Dietary Fibre 2 g; Cholesterol 77 mg; 1695 kJ (405 Cal)

Once the shiitake mushrooms have been soaked, thinly slice the caps.

CHINESE CLEAR SOUP WITH PORK BALLS AND EGG NOODLES

Preparation time: 25 minutes +
  overnight refrigeration +
  1 hour refrigeration
Cooking time: 4 hours
Serves 4–6

Stock
1.5 kg (3 lb 5 oz) chicken bones (chicken necks, backs, wings), washed
3 cloves garlic, sliced
2 slices ginger, 1 cm (1/2 inch) thick
4 spring onions (scallions), white part only

150 g (51/2 oz) Chinese cabbage (wom bok), shredded
1 tablespoon peanut oil
2 teaspoons sesame oil
4 cloves garlic, crushed
1 tablespoon grated ginger
300 g (101/2 oz) minced (ground) pork
1 egg white
1/4 teaspoon ground white pepper
2 tablespoons light soy sauce
1 tablespoon Chinese rice wine
11/2 tablespoons cornflour (cornstarch)
25 g (1/2 cup) coriander (cilantro) leaves, finely chopped
6 spring onions (scallions), finely sliced
200 g (7 oz) fresh fine egg noodles

1 To make the stock, put the bones and 3.5 litres (14 cups) water in a large saucepan and bring to a simmer—do not boil. Cook for 30 minutes, removing any scum that rises to the surface. Add the garlic, ginger and spring onion and cook, partially covered, at a low simmer for 3 hours. Strain through a fine sieve. Cool. Cover and refrigerate overnight.

Remove the layer of fat from the surface once it has solidified.
2 Bring a large saucepan of water to the boil and cook the cabbage for 2 minutes, or until soft. Drain, cool and squeeze out the excess water.
3 Heat the peanut oil and 1 teaspoon of the sesame oil in a small frying pan and cook the garlic and ginger for 1 minute, or until the garlic just starts to brown. Allow to cool.
4 Combine the pork, cabbage, garlic mixture, egg white, white pepper, soy sauce, rice wine, cornflour, half the coriander and half the spring onion. Cover and refrigerate for an hour. Shape into 22 balls using

1 tablespoon of mixture per ball.
5 Bring 1.5 litres (6 cups) of stock to the boil in a wok. Simmer for 1–2 minutes on medium heat. Add the pork balls and cook, covered, for 8–10 minutes, or until they rise to the top and are cooked through.
6 Cook the noodles in a large pan of boiling water for 1 minute. Drain and rinse. Divide among bowls and ladle the soup and balls on top. Garnish with the remaining spring onion, coriander and sesame oil.

NUTRITION PER SERVE (6)
Fat 9.5 g; Protein 17 g; Carbohydrate 23 g; Dietary Fibre 2 g; Cholesterol 34.5 mg; 1030 kJ (245 Cal)

Place all the meatball ingredients in a bowl and combine with your hands.

Once the pork balls have been shaped, add them to the wok one by one.

The pork balls are cooked when they rise to the surface.

PRAWN WON TONS WITH FRAGRANT COCONUT AND LEMON GRASS SOUP

Preparation time: 30 minutes +
  overnight refrigeration
Cooking time: 1 hour 10 minutes
Serves 4

Chicken stock

1.5 kg (3 lb 5 oz) chicken bones (chicken
  necks, backs, wings), washed
1 onion, roughly chopped
125 g (½ cup) roughly chopped
  celery

Prawn won tons

325 g (11½ oz) small prawns (shrimp)
2 tablespoons finely chopped
  coriander (cilantro) leaves
1 tablespoon shredded
  Thai basil
2 tablespoons finely chopped
  Chinese celery or celery
2 spring onions (scallions), finely
  chopped
20 won ton wrappers
1 egg, lightly beaten

2 tablespoons tom yum paste
  (see Note)
3 stems lemon grass
  (white part only), thinly sliced
6 makrut (kaffir) lime leaves
2 small red chillies, finely chopped
200 ml (7 fl oz) coconut milk
1 tablespoon grated palm
  sugar
1 tablespoon lime juice
1 tablespoon fish sauce
coriander (cilantro) leaves,
  to garnish

1 To make the chicken stock, place the chicken bones, chopped onion, celery and 3 litres (12 cups) water in a large saucepan and bring slowly to a simmer over medium heat. Skim off any scum that rises to the surface of the stock. Reduce the heat and simmer for about 1 hour, skimming the surface as necessary. Strain the stock through a fine sieve and allow to cool. Cover and refrigerate overnight. Remove the layer of fat from the surface.

2 To make the prawn won tons, peel the prawns, discarding the heads and tails. Gently pull out the dark vein from the backs, starting at the head end. Finely chop the prawns until almost minced, then combine with the coriander leaves, Thai basil, Chinese celery and chopped spring onion.

3 Place a heaped teaspoon of the prawn mixture in the centre of a won ton wrapper and lightly brush the edges with a little of the beaten egg. Lift the sides up tightly and pinch around the filling to form a pouch. Repeat with the remaining wrappers and filling to make 20 in total. Cover with plastic wrap and transfer to the fridge to chill.

4 Heat a wok over medium heat, add the tom yum paste and cook for 10 seconds, or until fragrant. Gradually whisk in 1 litre (4 cups) of the stock until combined, then bring to the boil over high heat. Reduce the heat to medium, then add the lemon grass, makrut lime leaves, chilli and coconut milk, and simmer for 5 minutes. Stir in the palm sugar, lime juice and fish sauce. Gently add the won tons to the broth and

simmer for 2–3 minutes, or until cooked through. Remove the won tons with a slotted spoon and place five in each serving bowl. Ladle on the broth and garnish with the coriander leaves. Serve at once.

NUTRITION PER SERVE
Fat 14 g; Protein 22 g; Carbohydrate 34 g; Dietary Fibre 2 g; Cholesterol 114.5 mg; 1400 kJ (335 Cal)

COOK'S FILE
Note: Tom yum paste is an excellent base flavour for soups and other Asian dishes. It is made from garlic, chilli, galangal, makrut (kaffir) lime leaves, lemon grass and shrimp paste. For vegetarian cooking, make sure you buy a brand that does not include shrimp paste or fish sauce.

Gently pull the dark vein from the prawn backs, starting at the head end.

Seal the won tons by gathering the wrapper around the filling to form a pouch.

HOT AND SOUR SOUP WITH NOODLES

Preparation time: 40 minutes +
  overnight refrigeration +
  10 minutes standing
Cooking time: 4 hours 30 minutes
Serves 6

Stock
1.5 kg (3 lb 5 oz) chicken bones (chicken
  necks, backs, wings), washed
2 slices ginger, 1 cm (1/2 inch) thick
4 spring onions (scallions), white
  part only

200 g (7 oz) chicken breast fillet, cut
  into 2 cm (3/4 inch) pieces
2 tablespoons garlic and red chilli
  paste
60 ml (1/4 cup) light soy sauce
3/4 teaspoon ground white pepper
115 g (4 oz) baby corn, quartered
  lengthways
80 ml (1/3 cup) Chinese black
  vinegar
4 fresh shiitake mushrooms, stems
  removed, caps thinly sliced
100 g (31/2 oz) enoki mushrooms,
  trimmed and separated

65 g (21/4 oz) fresh black wood fungus,
  cut into 1 cm (1/2 inch) strips
200 g (7 oz) fresh Shanghai noodles
200 g (7 oz) firm tofu, cut into 2.5 cm
  (1/4 inch) cubes
3 tablespoons cornflour (cornstarch)
3 eggs, lightly beaten
1 teaspoon sesame oil
2 spring onions (scallions), thinly
  sliced on the diagonal

1 To make the stock, place the bones and 3.5 litres (14 cups) water in a large saucepan and simmer—do not boil. Cook for 30 minutes, removing any scum as it rises to the surface. Add the ginger and spring onion and cook, partially covered, at a low simmer for 3 hours. Strain through a fine sieve and allow to cool. Cover and refrigerate overnight. Remove the layer of fat from the surface.
2 To make the soup, bring 2 litres (8 cups) of the stock to the boil in a large saucepan over high heat (freeze any remaining stock). Reduce the heat to medium, add the chicken, garlic and chilli paste, soy sauce and white pepper and stir to combine. Simmer, covered, for 10 minutes, or

until the chicken is cooked. Add the corn, vinegar, mushrooms, wood fungus, noodles and tofu. Season with salt and gently simmer for 5 minutes—do not stir.
3 Combine the cornflour and 60 ml (1/4 cup) water. Slowly stir into the soup until combined and slightly thickened. Return to a simmer. Pour the egg over the surface in a very thin stream. Turn off the heat, stand for 10 minutes. Stir in the sesame oil. Garnish with the spring onion.

NUTRITION PER SERVE
Fat 9.5 g; Protein 23 g; Carbohydrate 31 g; Dietary Fibre 3.5 g; Cholesterol 127.5 mg; 1265 kJ (300 Cal)

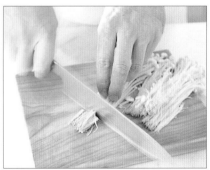

Cut the ends off the enoki mushrooms, then separate the stems.

BEEF PHO

Preparation time: 15 minutes +
    40 minutes freezing
Cooking time: 30 minutes
Serves 4

400 g (14 oz) rump steak, trimmed
1 litre (4 cups) beef stock
1/2 onion
1 star anise
1 cinnamon stick
1 tablespoon fish sauce
pinch ground white pepper
200 g (7 oz) fresh thin round rice noodles
2 spring onions (scallions), thinly
    sliced
30 Vietnamese mint leaves
90 g (3 1/4 oz) bean sprouts
1 small white onion, thinly sliced
1 small red chilli, thinly sliced

1 Wrap the meat in plastic wrap and freeze for 30–40 minutes, or until partially frozen. Thinly slice the meat across the grain.

2 Place the stock in a large heavy-based saucepan with the onion half, star anise, cinnamon stick, fish sauce, white pepper and 500 ml (2 cups) water and bring to the boil over high heat. Reduce the heat to medium–low and simmer, covered, for 20 minutes. Discard the onion, star anise and cinnamon stick.

3 Meanwhile, cover the noodles with boiling water and gently separate. Drain and refresh with cold water. Divide the noodles and spring onion among the serving bowls. Top with equal amounts of beef, mint, bean sprouts, onion slices and chilli. Ladle on the simmering broth and serve.

NUTRITION PER SERVE
Fat 5.5 g; Protein 28 g; Carbohydrate 24 g;
Dietary Fibre 2 g; Cholesterol 64 mg;
1100 kJ (265 Cal)

COOK'S FILE
Note: It is important that the broth is kept hot as the heat will cook the slices of beef.

Thinly slice the partially frozen steak across the grain.

LONG AND SHORT NOODLE SOUP

Preparation time: 30 minutes
Cooking time: 15 minutes
Serves 6

300 g (10½ oz) minced (ground) pork
4 spring onions (scallions), sliced
3 cloves garlic, roughly chopped
2 teaspoons grated ginger
2 teaspoons cornflour (cornstarch)
110 ml (3¾ fl oz) light soy sauce
3 tablespoons Chinese rice wine
30 won ton wrappers
3 litres (12 cups) ready-made Chinese chicken broth (see Notes)
200 g (7 oz) dried flat egg noodles
2 spring onions (scallions), extra, sliced on the diagonal
1 teaspoon sesame oil

1 Place the minced pork, spring onion, garlic, ginger, cornflour, 1½ tablespoons of the soy sauce and 1 tablespoon of the rice wine in a food processor and process until the mixture is well combined.
2 Place 2 teaspoons of the mixture in the centre of a won ton wrapper and lightly brush the edges with water. Lift the sides up tightly and pinch around the filling to form a pouch. Repeat with the remaining filling and wrappers to make 30 won tons in total.
3 Place the chicken broth in a large saucepan and bring to a simmer over medium–high heat. Stir in the remaining soy sauce and rice wine.
4 Meanwhile, bring a large saucepan of water to the boil. Reduce the heat, add the won tons and simmer for 1 minute, or until they float to the surface and are cooked through. Remove the won tons with a slotted spoon. Return the water to the boil, add the egg noodles and cook for 3 minutes, or until tender. Drain and add to the chicken broth along with the cooked won tons, simmering for 2 minutes, or until heated through.
5 Divide the broth, noodles and won tons among six large serving bowls, sprinkle with extra spring onion and drizzle each with a little sesame oil, to taste.

NUTRITION PER SERVE
Fat 8.5 g; Protein 25.5 g; Carbohydrate 57.5 g; Dietary Fibre 5 g; Cholesterol 65 mg; 1785 kJ (425 Cal)

COOK'S FILE
Notes: Chinese chicken broth is available in cans in Asian grocery stores and in the Asian section of some large supermarkets. If it's not available, you can use home-made or bought chicken stock instead.
For a more traditional dumpling, use 200 g (7 oz) minced (ground) pork and 100 g (3½ oz) minced (ground) prawn (shrimp).

Twist the edges of the won ton wrappers together to seal and enclose the filling.

CHICKEN AND NOODLE SOUP

Preparation time: 10 minutes
Cooking time: 35 minutes
Serves 6

1.5 litres (6 cups) chicken stock
  (see Note)
1 star anise
4 slices ginger (5 mm or ¼ inch thick)
400 g (14 oz) chicken breast fillets
375 g (13 oz) Shanghai noodles
1 tablespoon Chinese rice wine
1 tablespoon julienned ginger
1½ tablespoons light soy sauce
½ teaspoon sugar
155 g (5½ oz) asparagus, cut into
  3 cm (1¼ inch) lengths
4 spring onions (scallions), white
  and some green parts, thinly sliced
  on diagonal
50 g (1¾ oz) watercress, tips picked
  off the stems
¼ teaspoon sesame oil
light soy sauce, extra, to serve

1 Place the stock in a large saucepan and bring to the boil over high heat. Reduce to medium–low, add the star anise, ginger slices and chicken and simmer for 15–20 minutes, or until the chicken is cooked through. Remove the chicken with a slotted spoon and set aside to cool. Discard the star anise and ginger, reserving the stock in the pan.

2 Meanwhile, bring 2 litres (8 cups) water to the boil in a large saucepan. Cook the noodles for 4–5 minutes. Drain immediately, then rinse under cold water to refresh.

3 Cut the chicken across the breast into 5 mm (¼ inch) slices. Return the stock to the boil over high heat. Add the rice wine, julienned ginger, soy sauce, sugar, asparagus and ½ teaspoon salt, stirring to combine. Reduce the heat to medium, add the noodles and simmer for 2 minutes. Return the chicken to the pan and cook for a further 1 minute, or until heated through.

4 Gently remove the noodles from the soup with tongs. Evenly divide among six serving bowls. Spoon the chicken, asparagus, spring onion and

watercress into bowls, then ladle on the stock. Drizzle with sesame oil and serve with extra soy sauce, if desired.

NUTRITION PER SERVE
Fat 5.5 g; Protein 25.5 g; Carbohydrate 47 g; Dietary Fibre 2.5 g; Cholesterol 55 mg; 1450 kJ (345 Cal)

COOK'S FILE
Note: If using purchased ready-made stock, dilute 1 litre (4 cups) stock with 500 ml (2 cups) water—purchased stock is often salty.

Cut the ginger into even julienne strips, using a sharp knife.

MISO WITH RAMEN

Preparation time: 15 minutes +
   15 minutes soaking
Cooking time: 15 minutes
Serves 4

1 teaspoon finely chopped dried
   wakame
180 g (6 oz) fresh ramen noodles
100 g (3½ oz) silken firm tofu, cut
   into 1.5 cm (⅝ inch) cubes
2 spring onions (scallions), thinly
   sliced on the diagonal
1¾ teaspoons dashi powder
2–3 tablespoons red miso
   (see Note)
2 teaspoons mirin
2 teaspoon Japanese soy sauce

1 Soak the wakame in a bowl of
tepid water for 15 minutes. Drain
and set aside.

2 Cook the noodles in a large
saucepan of boiling salted water for
2 minutes, or until cooked through.
Drain and rinse, then divide among
four warmed serving bowls. Put the
tofu and spring onion on top.

3 Meanwhile, bring 1.25 litres
(5 cups) water to the boil in a large
saucepan. Reduce the heat to low and
add the dashi powder, stirring for
30 seconds, or until dissolved.

4 In a bowl, combine the miso with
250 ml (1 cup) of the dashi stock,
whisking until smooth. Return the
miso mixture to the saucepan and stir
until combined—be careful not to
boil the broth as this will diminish
the flavour of the miso. Add the
mirin, soy sauce and wakame and
gently heat for 1 minute, and stir to
combine. Ladle the broth over the
noodles, tofu and spring onion and
serve immediately.

NUTRITION PER SERVE
Fat 3 g; Protein 9 g; Carbohydrate 27.5 g;
Dietary Fibre 2.5 g; Cholesterol 6 mg;
735 kJ (175 Cal)

COOK'S FILE
Note: Shiro (white) miso can be used
instead of red miso, however the
flavour will not be as strong—adjust
to taste.

*Chop the wakame into fine pieces with a
sharp knife.*

EIGHT TREASURE NOODLE SOUP

Preparation time: 20 minutes +
20 minutes soaking
Cooking time: 20 minutes
Serves 4

10 g (¼ oz) dried shiitake mushrooms
375 g (13 oz) thick fresh egg noodles
1.25 litres (5 cups) good-quality
chicken stock
60 ml (¼ cup) light soy sauce
2 teaspoons Chinese rice wine
200 g (7 oz) chicken breast fillet, cut into
1 cm (½ inch) strips on the diagonal
200 g (7 oz) Chinese barbecued pork
(char siu), cut into 5 mm (¼ inch)
slices
¼ onion, finely chopped

1 carrot, cut into 1 cm (½ inch) slices
on the diagonal
120 g (4½ oz) snow peas (mangetout),
cut in half on the diagonal
4 spring onions (scallions), thinly sliced

1 Place the shiitake mushrooms in
a heatproof bowl, cover with boiling
water and soak for 20 minutes, or
until soft. Drain and squeeze out any
excess liquid. Discard the woody
stems and thinly slice the caps.
2 Bring a large saucepan of water to
the boil and cook the noodles for
1 minute, or until cooked through.
Drain, then rinse with cold water.
Divide evenly into four deep warmed
serving bowls.
3 Meanwhile, bring the chicken
stock to the boil in a large saucepan

over high heat. Reduce the heat to
medium and add the soy sauce and
rice wine, stirring to combine.
Simmer for 2 minutes. Add the
chicken and pork. Cook for another
2 minutes, or until the chicken is
cooked through and the pork is
heated. Add the onion, carrot, snow
peas, shiitake mushrooms and half
the spring onion. Cook for a further
1 minute, or until the carrot is tender.
4 Divide the vegetables and meat
among the serving bowls and ladle on
the hot broth. Garnish each bowl
with the remaining spring onion.

NUTRITION PER SERVE
Fat 7 g; Protein 41.5 g; Carbohydrate 61 g;
Dietary Fibre 4 g; Cholesterol 109 mg;
1995 kJ (475 Cal)

FISH BALL AND NOODLE SOUP

Preparation time: 20 minutes
Cooking time: 15 minutes
Serves 4–6

500 g (1 lb 2 oz) white firm fish fillets,
    skin and bones removed (ling or
    perch)
2 tablespoons rice flour
200 g (7 oz) dried somen noodles
2½ teaspoons dashi powder
2 tablespoons light soy sauce
1 tablespoon mirin
200 g (7 oz) Chinese cabbage,
    (wom bok) shredded
2 spring onions (scallions), thinly
    sliced on the diagonal
½ Lebanese (short) cucumber,
    unpeeled, seeded and cut thinly
    into 5 cm (2 inch) strips

1 Place the fish in a food processor and process until smooth. Combine the rice flour and 80 ml (¹⁄₃ cup) water in a small bowl and stir until smooth, then add to the fish and process for a further 5 seconds. Using 2 teaspoons of mixture at a time, shape into balls with wet hands.
2 Cook the somen noodles in a large saucepan of boiling water for 2 minutes, or until tender. Drain.
3 Pour 2 litres (8 cups) water into a large saucepan and bring to the boil. Reduce the heat to low, add the dashi powder and stir until dissolved. Bring the stock to the boil over high heat and add the soy sauce, mirin and salt to taste. Add the fish balls, reduce the heat to medium and simmer for 3 minutes, or until they rise to the surface and are cooked through. Add the cabbage, increase the heat to high and return to the boil. Stir in

the noodles and cook for 1 minute, or until warmed through.
4 To serve, divide the noodles and fish balls among serving bowls, then ladle the liquid on top. Garnish with the spring onion and cucumber.

NUTRITION PER SERVE (6)
Fat 2.5 g; Protein 22 g; Carbohydrate 27 g; Dietary Fibre 2 g; Cholesterol 49 mg; 930 kJ (220 Cal)

Place the cucumber over a small bowl, then remove the seeds with a spoon.

UDON NOODLES IN BROTH

Preparation time: 10 minutes
Cooking time: 15 minutes
Serves 4

2 teaspoons dashi powder
3 spring onions (scallions)
60 ml (¼ cup) mirin
60 ml (¼ cup) Japanese soy
    sauce
1 tablespoon sugar
400 g (14 oz) fresh udon noodles
shichimi togarashi, to garnish (optional)
    (see Note)

1 Pour 1.5 litres (6 cups) water into a large saucepan and bring to the boil. Reduce the heat to low, add the dashi powder and stir until dissolved.
2 Trim 2 spring onions then cut into 4 cm (1½ inch) pieces. Add to the dashi stock along with the mirin, soy sauce and sugar and stir to combine. Simmer, covered, over low heat for 5 minutes.
3 Meanwhile, cook the noodles in a saucepan of boiling water for 1–2 minutes, or until tender. Drain, refresh under cold water, then divide among four serving bowls. Slice the remaining spring onion thinly on the diagonal and place on top of the noodles. Ladle the liquid on top and sprinkle with a pinch of shichimi togarashi, if desired.

NUTRITION PER SERVE
Fat 0.5 g; Protein 5.5 g; Carbohydrate 31 g; Dietary Fibre 2 g; Cholesterol 0 mg; 690 kJ (165 Cal)

COOK'S FILE
Note: Shichimi togarashi is a popular seasoning mix in Japan. It translates as 'seven flavour chilli' and usually consists of ground chilli, plus a variety of six spices and seeds.

PORK AND BUTTERED CORN RAMEN SOUP

Preparation time: 15 minutes
Cooking time: 30 minutes
Serves 4

200 g (7 oz) Chinese barbecued pork
  (char siu), fillet in one piece
2 small corn cobs (550 g or 1 lb 4 oz)
200 g (7 oz) dried ramen noodles
2 teaspoons peanut oil
1 teaspoon grated ginger
1.5 litres (6 cups) chicken stock
2 tablespoons mirin
2 spring onions (scallions), sliced on
  the diagonal
20 g (1/2 oz) unsalted butter
1 spring onion (scallion), extra, sliced
  on the diagonal

1 Cut the pork into thin slices and remove the corn kernels from the cob using a sharp knife.
2 Cook the ramen noodles in a large saucepan of boiling water for 4 minutes, or until tender. Drain, then rinse in cold water.
3 Heat the oil in a large saucepan over high heat. Stir-fry the ginger for 1 minute. Add the chicken stock and mirin and bring to the boil. Reduce the heat and simmer for 8 minutes.
4 Add the pork slices to the liquid and cook for 5 minutes, then add the corn kernels and spring onion and cook for a further 4–5 minutes, or until the kernels are tender.
5 Separate the noodles by running them under hot water, then divide among four deep bowls. Ladle on the soup, then place 1 teaspoon butter on each serving. Garnish with the extra spring onion and serve at once.

NUTRITION PER SERVE
Fat 10.5 g; Protein 23 g; Carbohydrate 41.5 g; Dietary Fibre 3 g; Cholesterol 76.5 mg; 1510 kJ (360 Cal)

COOK'S FILE
Note: This soup is traditionally served with the butter on top. However, for a healthier option, it is also quite delicious without the butter.

Cut the barbecued pork into thin slices, using a small sharp knife.

Remove the kernels from the corn cobs by cutting down the cob with a knife.

Cut the incisions on the underside of each peeled prawn.

Gently dip each prawn into the tempura batter, leaving the tail uncoated.

Deep-fry the prawns a few at a time until crispy and cooked through.

TEMPURA PRAWNS WITH UDON NOODLES AND DASHI BROTH

Preparation time: 20 minutes
Cooking time: 15 minutes
Serves 4 as a starter

500 g (1 lb 2 oz) fresh udon noodles
1 spring onion (scallion), sliced on the diagonal
60 g (2¼ oz) daikon, cut into thin strips
1 teaspoon dashi granules
60 ml (¼ cup) Japanese soy sauce
2 tablespoons mirin
½ teaspoon caster (superfine) sugar
2 spring onions (scallions), extra, thinly sliced on the diagonal
2 teaspoons black sesame seeds
shredded pickled ginger, to garnish

Tempura prawns
12 medium king prawns (shrimp)
oil, to deep-fry

125 g (1 cup) tempura flour
250 ml (1 cup) iced water

1 Cook the udon noodles in a large saucepan of boiling water for 1–2 minutes, or until tender. Drain and rinse, then add the spring onion and daikon, toss well and keep warm.
2 To make the broth, place the dashi granules, soy sauce, mirin, sugar and 500 ml (2 cups) water in a saucepan and bring to the boil. Reduce the heat to medium and simmer for 2–3 minutes. Remove from the heat, cover and keep warm.
3 To make the tempura prawns, peel and devein the prawns, keeping the tails intact. Make four incisions in the underside of each prawn.
4 Fill a wok or deep heavy-based saucepan one-third full of oil and heat to 180°C (350°F), or until a cube of bread dropped into the oil browns in 15 seconds. Combine the tempura flour with the iced water

and mix briefly with chopsticks or a fork—the batter should still be lumpy. Dip each prawn into the batter, leaving the tail uncoated. Deep-fry in batches for about 30 seconds, or until the prawns are lightly golden, crisp and cooked through. Drain well on paper towels.
5 Divide the noodles among the serving bowls and cover with broth and the extra spring onion. Top each bowl with three prawns and sprinkle with the sesame seeds. Garnish with the pickled ginger and serve at once.

NUTRITION PER SERVE
Fat 6.5 g; Protein 14.5 g; Carbohydrate 40.5 g; Dietary Fibre 3 g; Cholesterol 53 mg; 1220 kJ (290 Cal)

SICHUAN BEEF NOODLE SOUP

Preparation time: 10 minutes +
   5 minutes standing
Cooking time: 2 hours 15 minutes
Serves 4

1.25 litres (5 cups) beef stock
1 tablespoon peanut oil
400 g (14 oz) piece chuck steak
2 star anise
½ cinnamon stick
1½ teaspoons Sichuan peppercorns,
   crushed
1 tablespoon julienned ginger
2 tablespoons dark soy sauce
1 tablespoon Chinese rice wine
1 tablespoon brown bean paste
1 piece dried mandarin peel (about
   5 cm x 3 cm or 2 inch x 1¼ inch)
125 g (4½ oz) fresh thin egg noodles
3 spring onions (scallions), thinly
   sliced on the diagonal

1 Preheat the oven to hot 220°C (425°F/Gas 7). Pour the beef stock and 1.25 litres (5 cups) water into a large saucepan and warm over low heat.

2 Heat the peanut oil in a frying pan. Add the steak and sear for 2–3 minutes on each side. Transfer to a 3 litre (12 cup) claypot or casserole dish and add the star anise, cinnamon stick, crushed peppercorns, ginger, soy sauce, rice wine, bean paste and dried mandarin peel. Pour in the hot broth, then cover and bake for 2 hours, or until the steak is tender (you should be able to shred it; if not, return to the oven and cook until tender).

3 Remove the steak and set aside. Discard the mandarin peel. Add the noodles to the broth, cover and allow to stand for 1–2 minutes, or until the noodles are soft. Shred the steak into bite-size pieces and divide evenly among four large serving bowls. Ladle the broth and noodles on top, sprinkle with the spring onion and serve immediately.

NUTRITION PER SERVE
Fat 9.5 g; Protein 28.5 g; Carbohydrate 20 g; Dietary Fibre 1.5 g; Cholesterol 61 mg; 1190 kJ (285 Cal)

Crush the Sichuan peppercorns in a mortar and pestle.

Using your hands, shred the tender steak into bite-size pieces.

VIETNAMESE FISH AND CELLOPHANE NOODLE SOUP

Preparation time: 30 minutes +
    5 minutes soaking
Cooking time: 25 minutes
Serves 4

1 teaspoon shrimp paste
150 g (5½ oz) mung bean vermicelli
2 tablespoons peanut oil
6 cloves garlic, finely chopped
1 small onion, thinly sliced
2 long red chillies, chopped
2 stems lemon grass (white part only),
    thinly sliced
1.25 litres (5 cups) chicken stock
3 tablespoons fish sauce
1 tablespoon rice vinegar
4 ripe tomatoes, peeled, seeded
    and chopped
500 g (1 lb 2 oz) firm white fish fillets
    (snapper or blue-eye cod), cut into
    3 cm (1¼ inch) pieces
25 g (½ cup) Vietnamese mint, torn
15 g (½ cup) coriander (cilantro)
    leaves
90 g (1 cup) bean sprouts
1 tablespoon Vietnamese mint, extra
1 tablespoon coriander (cilantro)
    leaves, extra
2 long red chillies, extra, sliced
lemon wedges, to serve

1 Wrap the shrimp paste in foil and put under a hot grill for 1 minute. Remove and set aside until needed.
2 Place the vermicelli in a heatproof bowl, cover with boiling water and soak for 3–4 minutes. Rinse under cold water, drain and then cut into 15 cm (6 inch) lengths.
3 Heat the peanut oil in a heavy-based saucepan over medium heat. Add the garlic and cook for 1 minute, or until golden. Add the onion, chilli, lemon grass and shrimp paste and cook, stirring, for a further minute. Pour in the stock, fish sauce and rice vinegar. Add the tomato. Bring to the boil, then reduce the heat to medium and simmer for 10 minutes. Add the fish. Simmer gently for 3 minutes, or until cooked. Stir in the mint and coriander leaves.
4 Divide the noodles and bean

sprouts among four serving bowls and ladle the soup on top. Top with the extra mint, coriander leaves and chilli. Serve with lemon wedges.

NUTRITION PER SERVE
Fat 13 g; Protein 33 g; Carbohydrate 21 g;
Dietary Fibre 5.5 g; Cholesterol 73.5 mg;
1405 kJ (335 Cal)

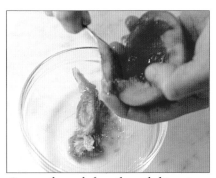

Remove the seeds from the peeled tomatoes with a spoon.

Simmer the fish pieces in the soup until cooked.

25

VIETNAMESE FRESH SPRING ROLLS

Preparation time: 40 minutes +
  10 minutes soaking
Cooking time: Nil
Makes 20

Dipping sauce
60 ml (¼ cup) sweet chilli sauce
1 tablespoon lime juice

100 g (3½ oz) dried rice vermicelli
½ green mango, julienned
1 small Lebanese (short) cucumber, julienned
½ avocado, cut into thin strips
4 spring onions (scallions), thinly sliced
15 g (½ cup) coriander (cilantro) leaves
2 tablespoons chopped Vietnamese mint
1 tablespoon sweet chilli sauce
2 tablespoons lime juice
20 square (15 cm or 6 inch) rice paper wrappers

1 To make the dipping sauce, put the sweet chilli sauce and lime juice in a small bowl and mix well.
2 To make the fresh spring rolls, place the vermicelli in a heatproof bowl, cover with boiling water and soak for 6–7 minutes, or until softened. Drain well, then cut into 10 cm (4 inch) lengths.
3 Combine the vermicelli, mango, cucumber, avocado, spring onion, coriander leaves, mint, sweet chilli sauce and lime juice in a bowl.
4 Working with one rice paper wrapper at a time, dip each wrapper in a bowl of warm water for 10 seconds to soften, then lay out on a flat work surface. Place 1 tablespoon of the filling on the wrapper, fold in the sides and roll up tightly. Repeat with the remaining filling and rice paper wrappers to make 20 in total. Serve the rolls immediately with the dipping sauce.

NUTRITION PER ROLL
Fat 1.5 g; Protein 1 g; Carbohydrate 6.5 g; Dietary Fibre 0.5 g; Cholesterol 0 mg; 180 kJ (45 Cal)

COOK'S FILE
Note: Ensure the rice paper rolls are rolled tightly together or they will fall apart while you eat them.
Storage: Although these rolls are best eaten straight away, you can make them 2–3 hours ahead of time. Layer them between baking paper or plastic wrap and store in an airtight container to prevent them drying out.

Place all the filling ingredients in a bowl and mix together until well combined.

Fold in the sides of the wrapper and roll up tightly.

RICE NOODLE PANCAKES WITH ROAST DUCK

Preparation time: 20 minutes +
 5 minutes soaking
Cooking time: 30 minutes
Serves 4–6

½ Chinese roast duck (1.4 kg or
 3 lb 2 oz)
400 g (14 oz) fresh flat rice noodles
 (about 5 mm or ¼ inch wide)
2 small red chillies, seeded
 and finely chopped
3 spring onions (scallions), thinly
 sliced
1 teaspoon peanut oil
250 ml (1 cup) vegetable oil
60 ml (¼ cup) hoisin sauce
1 Lebanese (short) cucumber, seeded
 and julienned
2 spring onions (scallions), extra,
 julienned into 5 cm (2 inch) lengths
coriander (cilantro) leaves, to garnish

1 Preheat the oven to moderate 180°C (350°F/Gas 4). Remove the legs and wings from the duck by twisting the joints away from the body and cutting through the bones. Carefully ease the skin and flesh away from the carcass in one piece, trimming away any excess fat. Place the flesh on a baking tray.
2 Cut the noodles into 10 cm (4 inch) long pieces. Place in a large heatproof bowl, cover with boiling water and soak briefly, gently separating with your fingers. Drain, rinse with cold water and drain again. Put the noodles on paper towels to drain away any excess moisture.
3 Combine the noodles, chilli, spring onion and the peanut oil in a large bowl. Heat the vegetable oil in a large heavy-based frying pan over high heat. Pour 3 tablespoons of the noodle mixture per pancake into the pan and cook for 2–3 minutes on each side, or until crispy and golden brown. Drain on paper towels. Repeat with the remaining mixture to make 12 pancakes in total.
4 Meanwhile, roast the duck for 10 minutes, or until the skin is crispy. Cut into 1 cm (¼ inch) thick strips. Spread the hoisin sauce onto each pancake, add some cucumber and spring onion and top with slices of duck. Garnish with coriander leaves.

NUTRITION PER SERVE (6)
Fat 21 g; Protein 13 g; Carbohydrate 32 g;
Dietary Fibre 2 g; Cholesterol 61 mg;
1550 kJ (370 Cal)

Carefully ease the skin and flesh away from the duck carcass.

Fry the pancakes on both sides until crispy and golden.

Trim around the edge of the lettuce leaves to neaten the cups.

Add the mushrooms, capsicum, bean sprouts and water chestnuts to the wok.

Stir the noodles and coriander through the minced meat mixture in the wok.

CHICKEN AND PORK MINCE WITH FRIED NOODLES IN LETTUCE CUPS

Preparation time: 15 minutes +
    20 minutes soaking
Cooking time: 10 minutes
Serves 4

4 dried Chinese mushrooms
8 iceberg lettuce leaves
1 tablespoon peanut oil
2 cloves garlic, crushed
2 teaspoons grated ginger
6 spring onions (scallions), thinly
    sliced
200 g (7 oz) minced (ground) pork
200 g (7 oz) minced (ground) chicken
1/2 red capsicum (pepper), diced
50 g (1 3/4 oz) bean sprouts
70 g (1/2 cup) water chestnuts, diced
2 tablespoons oyster sauce

1 1/2 teaspoons soy sauce
2 tablespoons dry sherry
1/2 teaspoon sugar
50 g (1 3/4 oz) purchased fried noodles
4 tablespoons coriander (cilantro)
    leaves

1 Place the dried mushrooms in a heatproof bowl, cover with boiling water and soak for 20 minutes. Drain, then remove the woody stems. Squeeze out any excess liquid and thinly slice the caps. Sit one lettuce leaf inside another leaf to make four cups. Trim the edges to neaten, then refrigerate until needed.

2 Heat the oil in a wok over high heat. Add the garlic, ginger and half the spring onion and stir-fry for 30 seconds. Add the minced pork and chicken and cook for 3–4 minutes, or until cooked through, breaking up any lumps. Add the capsicum, bean sprouts, water chestnuts and mushrooms and stir-fry for 1 minute. Add the oyster and soy sauces, sherry, sugar and the remaining spring onion and cook, tossing, for 2–3 minutes, or until thickened and reduced slightly. Stir in the noodles and coriander and divide among the lettuce cups. Serve immediately.

NUTRITION PER SERVE
Fat 13 g; Protein 22 g; Carbohydrate 10 g; Dietary Fibre 2.5 g; Cholesterol 75.5 mg; 1060 kJ (255 Cal)

COOK'S FILE
Note: It is important to stir the fried noodles through just before serving so they retain some of their crunch.

SPICY PRAWN FRITTERS

Preparation time: 25 minutes
Cooking time: 15 minutes
Makes 24

Dipping sauce
3 tablespoons sweet chilli sauce
2 tablespoons lime juice

200 g (7 oz) fresh egg noodles
500 g (1 lb 2 oz) small peeled prawns
    (shrimp) (Royal reds), patted dry
    and finely chopped
4 tablespoons finely chopped
    coriander (cilantro) leaves
2 cloves garlic, crushed
5 spring onions (scallions), finely
    chopped
1 small red chilli, finely
    chopped
2 makrut (kaffir) lime leaves, finely
    chopped
2 teaspoons fish sauce
1 tablespoon sweet chilli sauce
1 egg, lightly beaten
oil, to shallow-fry

1 To make the dipping sauce, combine the sweet chilli sauce and lime juice in a bowl.
2 Cook the noodles in a large saucepan of boiling water for 1 minute, then drain and rinse. Cut into 5 cm (2 inch) lengths.
3 Place the prawns, coriander leaves, garlic, spring onion, chilli, lime leaves, fish sauce, sweet chilli sauce and egg in a bowl and mix until well combined. Add the noodles and mix with your hands until well combined. Using heaped tablespoons, form the mixture into 24 fritters.

4 Fill a large frying pan to 1 cm (1/2 inch) deep with oil and heat to 180°C (350°F), or until a cube of bread browns in 15 seconds. Fry the fritters in three batches for 3–4 minutes each batch, or until cooked through and golden and crispy on the outside. Drain on paper towels. Serve immediately with the dipping sauce.

NUTRITION PER FRITTER
Fat 3.5 g; Protein 5.5 g; Carbohydrate 5.5 g; Dietary Fibre 0.5 g; Cholesterol 40.5 mg; 315 kJ (75 Cal)

Mix the prawns, coriander, garlic, spring onion, chilli, lime leaves, sauces and egg.

Fry the fritters, in batches, on both sides until crispy and golden.

GYOZA

Preparation time: 50 minutes +
    30 minutes standing
Cooking time: 25 minutes
Makes 40

150 g (5¹/2 oz) Chinese cabbage
    (wom bok), very finely shredded
225 g (8 oz) minced (ground) pork
2 cloves garlic, finely chopped
2 teaspoons finely chopped ginger
2 spring onions (scallions), finely
    chopped
2 teaspoons cornflour (cornstarch)
1 tablespoon light soy sauce
2 teaspoons Chinese rice wine
2 teaspoons sesame oil
40 round Shanghai dumpling (flour
    and water) wrappers
2 tablespoons vegetable oil
125 ml (¹/2 cup) chicken stock

1 Place the cabbage and ¹/2 teaspoon salt in a colander, then sit in a larger bowl and toss to combine. Leave for 30 minutes to drain. Stir occasionally.
2 Place the minced pork, garlic, ginger, spring onion, cornflour, soy sauce, rice wine and sesame oil in a bowl and combine with your hands.
3 Rinse the cabbage under cold running water. Place between paper towels and press to absorb the excess moisture. Add to the pork mixture and combine well.
4 Place a teaspoon of mixture in the centre of a wrapper, brushing the inside edge of the wrapper with a little water. Bring the two edges of the wrapper together to form a semicircle. Using your thumb and index finger, create a pleat, pressing firmly as you do and gently tapping the gyoza on a work surface to form a flat bottom. Repeat with the remaining wrappers and filling to make 40 gyoza in total.
5 Heat a quarter of the oil in a large frying pan over medium–high heat. Cook a batch of 10 gyozas for 2 minutes, flat-side down. Reduce the heat and add a quarter of the stock to the pan, shaking the pan to unstick the gyoza. Cover, and cook for 4 minutes, or until the liquid has evaporated. Remove and keep warm. Repeat with the remaining oil, gyoza and stock. Serve with soy or Chinese black vinegar, if desired.

NUTRITION PER GYOZA
Fat 1.5 g; Protein 1.5 g; Carbohydrate
3.5 g; Dietary Fibre 0.5 g; Cholesterol
3.5 mg; 145 kJ (35 Cal)

Gently fold the edges of the wrapper with your fingers to create a pleat.

Cook the gyoza, in batches, in a large frying pan with oil.

SPRING ROLLS

Preparation time: 30 minutes +
   25 minutes soaking
Cooking time: 25 minutes
Makes 20

4 dried shiitake mushrooms
80 g (3 oz) dried rice vermicelli
1 tablespoon peanut oil
2 cloves garlic, chopped
2 teaspoons grated ginger
250 g (9 oz) (ground) pork
250 g (9 oz) medium prawns (shrimp),
   peeled and finely chopped
1 tablespoon light soy sauce
1 tablespoon oyster sauce
1 tablespoon Chinese rice wine
1 carrot, grated
8 water chestnuts, finely chopped
4 spring onions (scallions), thinly
   sliced
200 g (7 oz) Chinese cabbage
   (wom bok), finely shredded
1 tablespoon sweet chilli sauce
2 teaspoons cornflour (cornstarch)
20 large spring roll wrappers
oil, to deep-fry

1 Place the mushrooms in a small heatproof bowl, cover with boiling water and soak for 20 minutes. Drain and squeeze out the excess water. Discard the woody stems and thinly slice the caps. Place the vermicelli in a heatproof bowl, cover with boiling water and soak for 6–7 minutes, or until soft and transparent. Drain and cut into 5 cm (2 inch) lengths.
2 Heat the oil in a wok over high heat and swirl to coat. Add the garlic and ginger, and cook for 1 minute. Add the minced pork and cook for another 3 minutes, stirring to break up any lumps. Add the prawns and cook for 1 minute, or until they just turn pink. Stir in the soy sauce, oyster sauce, rice wine, carrot, water chestnuts, spring onion, Chinese cabbage and sweet chilli sauce and cook for 2 minutes, or until warmed through. Season to taste with salt and freshly ground black pepper. Stir in the mushrooms and vermicelli.
3 Combine the cornflour and 2 tablespoons water in a small bowl until smooth.
4 Place the spring roll wrappers under a damp tea towel. Working with one at a time, place a wrapper on the work surface with one corner facing you. Place 2 tablespoons of the filling along the centre of each spring roll wrapper. Brush the edges with the cornflour paste and roll up firmly, tucking in the ends as you go, and sealing with the cornflour paste. Continue, covering the completed rolls with a damp tea towel to prevent them drying out.
5 Fill a wok one-third full of oil and heat to 180°C (350°F), or until a cube of bread browns in 15 seconds. Cook the spring rolls in batches of 2–3 rolls, turning gently to brown evenly, for 2 minutes, or until golden. Drain on crumpled paper towels. Serve with light soy sauce or your favourite dipping sauce.

NUTRITION PER ROLL
Fat 2 g; Protein 7.5 g; Carbohydrate 14.5 g; Dietary Fibre 1 g; Cholesterol 27 mg; 460 kJ (110 Cal)

COOK'S FILE
Note: If the rolls are too big, serve cut in half on the diagonal.

Using your fingers, lightly wet the edges of the wrapper with the cornflour paste.

Roll up the spring roll, tucking in the sides, then seal with the cornflour paste.

PRAWN GOW GEES

Preparation time: 40 minutes +
  1 hour refrigeration
Cooking time: 15 minutes
Makes 24

300 g (10½ oz) medium prawns
  (shrimp), peeled, deveined and
  finely chopped
100 g (3½ oz) minced (ground) pork
4 spring onions (scallions), white part
  only, finely chopped
25 g (1 oz) bamboo shoots, finely
  chopped
1 egg white
1 teaspoon finely chopped ginger
1 teaspoon sesame oil
¼ teaspoon ground white pepper
24 round gow gee wrappers

Dipping sauce
60 ml (¼ cup) light soy sauce
1 tablespoon Chinese red vinegar
  (see Note)
¼ teaspoon sesame oil

1 To make the filling, mix the prawns, minced pork, spring onion, bamboo shoots, egg white, ginger, sesame oil, white pepper and 1 teaspoon salt in a bowl until well combined. Cover with plastic wrap and refrigerate for 1 hour.
2 Put one gow gee wrapper on a work surface and place 2 level teaspoons of the filling in the centre—position the filling in an oblong shape across the wrapper, rather than a round lump. Lightly moisten the edge of the wrapper with water. Pick up the wrapper and fold the edges together to form a semicircle. Using your thumb and index finger, create a row of pleats along the outside edge of the gow gee, pressing firmly. Twist the corners down to seal and form a crescent shape. Make sure the gow gee is completely sealed or the filling will leak out during steaming. Repeat with the remaining wrappers and filling to make 24 gow gees in total.
3 Line a 28 cm (11 inch) bamboo steamer with baking paper and arrange the gow gees so they do not touch—you will need to do this in

two batches (or use a double bamboo steamer). Place over a wok of simmering water, making sure the base of the steamer doesn't touch the water. Cover and steam for 8 minutes, or until cooked through.
4 To make the dipping sauce, combine the soy sauce, red vinegar and sesame oil. Serve with the gow gees.

NUTRITION PER GOW GEE
Fat 0.5 g; Protein 4.5 g; Carbohydrate 5 g; Dietary Fibre 0.5 g; Cholesterol 22.5 mg; 190 kJ (45 Cal)

COOK'S FILE
Note: Chinese red vinegar is a type of rice vinegar often used as a condiment. It is available from Asian grocery stores.

Create pleats in the gow gee wrapper, starting from the centre of the gow gee.

Using your fingers, gently bend the gow gee to form a crescent shape.

Push the flesh down the bone toward the joint, using a small, sharp knife.

Twist and pull the cleaned, exposed bone from the socket.

Using your fingers, stuff each chicken wing with a ball of mixture.

STUFFED CHICKEN WINGS

Preparation time: 30 minutes + cooling time
Cooking time: 20 minutes
Makes 12

12 large chicken wings
20 g (1 oz) dried rice vermicelli
1 tablespoon grated palm sugar
2 tablespoons fish sauce
200 g (7 oz) minced (ground) pork
2 spring onions (scallions), chopped
3 cloves garlic, chopped
1 small red chilli, chopped
3 tablespoons chopped coriander (cilantro) leaves
peanut oil, to deep-fry
rice flour, well seasoned, to coat
sweet chilli sauce, to serve

1 Using a small sharp knife and starting at the fatter end of the wing, scrape down the bone, pushing the flesh and skin as you go until you reach the connecting joint. Twist and pull the exposed bone from its socket and discard the bone. Take care not to pierce the skin. Repeat with the remaining wings.

2 Meanwhile, soak the vermicelli in boiling water for 6–7 minutes. Drain and cut into 2 cm (3/4 inch) pieces with scissors. Stir the palm sugar and fish sauce together in a small bowl until the sugar has dissolved.

3 Combine the minced pork, spring onion, garlic, chilli and the fish sauce mixture in a food processor until well mixed. Transfer to a bowl, then stir in the coriander and vermicelli. Divide the mixture into 12 even-sized balls. Stuff each boned-out section of chicken wing with a ball of mixture and secure firmly with a toothpick.

4 Place the wings in a bamboo or metal steamer over a wok of simmering water—ensure the base of the steamer doesn't touch the water. Cover and steam for 8 minutes. Remove the wings from the steamer, then set aside to firm and cool.

5 Fill a deep heavy-based saucepan one-third full of oil and heat to 200°C (400°F), or until a cube of bread browns in 5 seconds. Coat the wings in the seasoned flour. Cook in batches for 3 minutes each batch, or until the wings are golden and cooked through. Drain on paper towels. Remove the toothpicks and serve with the sweet chilli sauce.

NUTRITION PER WING
Fat 9.5 g; Protein 12 g; Carbohydrate 2.5 g; Dietary Fibre 0.5 g; Cholesterol 52.5 mg; 605 kJ (145 Cal)

VIETNAMESE CREPES WITH PORK, PRAWNS, AND NOODLES

Preparation time: 45 minutes +
4 hours resting
Cooking time: 35 minutes
Serves 6

265 g (1¹/2 cups) rice flour
1 teaspoon baking powder
1¹/2 teaspoons sugar
¹/2 teaspoon ground turmeric
250 ml (1 cup) coconut milk
3 teaspoons peanut oil
lime wedges, to serve

Dipping sauce
1 tablespoon fish sauce
2 tablespoons lime juice
1 tablespoon caster (superfine) sugar
1 small red chilli, finely chopped

Salad
1 carrot, coarsely grated
120 g (4 oz) iceberg lettuce, shredded
1 Lebanese (short) cucumber, julienned
100 g (3¹/2 oz) bean sprouts
20 g (1 cup) mint
30 g (1 cup) coriander (cilantro) leaves

Filling
75 g (2¹/2 oz) mung bean vermicelli,
    broken
1 tablespoon peanut oil
1 large onion, thinly sliced
6 cloves garlic, crushed
200 g (7 oz) minced (ground) pork fillet
250 g (9 oz) prawns (shrimp), peeled,
    deveined and chopped
1 red capsicum (pepper), thinly sliced
75 g (3 oz) button mushrooms, thinly
    sliced
1 tablespoon light soy sauce

¹/4 teaspoon ground white pepper
4 spring onions (scallions), thinly sliced

1 To make the crepe batter, blend the rice flour, baking powder, sugar, turmeric, coconut milk, ¹/2 teaspoon salt and 250 ml (1 cup) water in a blender to a smooth batter. Cover and leave in a warm place for 2–4 hours.
2 Mix together all the dipping sauce ingredients in a small bowl.
3 Toss the salad ingredients together.
4 To make the filling, soak the vermicelli in boiling water for 3–4 minutes, or until soft. Drain. Heat a wok over high heat, add the oil and swirl to coat. Add the onion and cook for 2 minutes. Add the garlic, cooking for 30 seconds. Add the pork and cook for 2 minutes, or until browned. Stir in the prawns, capsicum and mushrooms and cook until the prawns change colour. Stir in the noodles, soy sauce, white pepper and spring onion.
5 To make the crepes, whisk the batter until smooth. Heat ¹/2 teaspoon of oil in a 30 cm (12 inch) non-stick frying pan. Pour 80 ml (¹/3 cup) of the batter into the centre of the pan, and swirl to spread to edges. Cook over medium heat for 1–2 minutes, or until golden and crispy. Turn and repeat on the other side. Repeat to make six crepes in total.
6 Place a portion of filling on half a crepe, folding the other side on top. Repeat with the remaining crepes and filling. Serve with the sauce, salad and lime.

NUTRITION PER SERVE
Fat 15.5 g; Protein 22.5 g; Carbohydrate 52.5 g; Dietary Fibre 4.5 g; Cholesterol 93.5 mg; 1840 kJ (440 Cal)

Pour the batter into the centre of the heated frying pan.

Fold the other side of the crepe over the filling.

NOODLE NESTS FILLED WITH BARBECUED PORK

Preparation time: 15 minutes
Cooking time: 20 minutes
Serves 6

200 g (7 oz) dried fine egg noodles
80 ml (⅓ cup) hoisin sauce
60 ml (¼ cup) chicken stock
2 tablespoons Chinese rice wine
1 tablespoon Chinese black vinegar
1 teaspoon sesame oil
1 small red chilli, seeded and
    chopped
1 tablespoon light soy sauce
peanut oil, to deep-fry
400 g (14 oz) Chinese barbecued pork
    (char siu), thinly sliced (see Note)
400 g (14 oz) choy sum, leaves
    trimmed and separated

1 Cook the egg noodles in a large saucepan of boiling water for 3 minutes, or until tender. Drain. Cool completely, then divide into six even portions.

2 Combine the hoisin sauce, stock, rice wine, black vinegar, sesame oil, chilli and soy sauce in a bowl.

3 Fill a wok one-third full of peanut oil and heat to 180°C (350°F), or until a cube of bread dropped into the oil browns in 15 seconds. Put a portion of noodles in a large Chinese wire strainer (about 15 cm or 6 inches in diameter), pressing down with a smaller wire strainer to make a well in the centre. Holding the two handles together, deep-fry for 2 minutes, or until crisp and golden. Carefully remove the nests with tongs and drain on crumpled paper towels. Repeat with the remaining noodles to make six nests in total.

4 Heat a large wok over medium heat, add the hoisin sauce mixture and bring to a simmer. Add the pork and choy sum and toss for 1–2 minutes, or until the pork is heated through and the greens have wilted. Divide among the nests and drizzle with any remaining sauce. Serve immediately.

NUTRITION PER SERVE
Fat 10.5 g; Protein 26 g; Carbohydrate 30 g; Dietary Fibre 3.5 g; Cholesterol 91.5 mg; 1375 kJ (330 Cal)

COOK'S FILE
Note: Chinese barbecued pork is available from Asian butchers, barbecue shops or restaurants and is best purchased on the day of eating. Do not microwave as it will toughen the meat.

Deep-fry the noodles between two wire strainers until crisp and golden.

SOBA NOODLE AND TUNA SUSHI

Preparation time: 35 minutes +
   20 minutes soaking
Cooking time: 15 minutes
Makes 36 pieces

6 dried shiitake mushrooms
125 ml (1/2 cup) dashi stock (see Note)
60 ml (1/4 cup) Japanese soy sauce
1 tablespoon mirin
1 tablespoon sugar
200 g (7 oz) dried soba noodles
2 tablespoons toasted black
   sesame seeds
6 sheets toasted nori
1 Lebanese (short) cucumber,
   cut into batons
200 g (7 oz) sashimi tuna, cut into
   1 cm (1/2 inch) wide strips
2 tablespoons shredded pickled ginger

Dipping sauce
1 teaspoon wasabi paste
60 ml (1/4 cup) Japanese soy sauce
2 teaspoons mirin

1 Place the shiitake mushrooms in a heatproof bowl, cover with boiling water and soak for 20 minutes, or until softened. Drain and squeeze out the excess liquid. Discard the stems and thinly slice the caps. Place the dashi stock, soy sauce, mirin and sugar in a saucepan and stir over low heat until the sugar has dissolved. Bring to the boil, add the mushrooms, then reduce the heat and simmer for 10 minutes, or until the liquid has almost completely evaporated. Strain in a colander without pressing the mushrooms.
2 Meanwhile, half fill a large saucepan with water and bring to the boil. Add the noodles and stir to separate. Return to the boil, then add 250 ml (1 cup) cold water. Repeat this step 3 times as the water just comes to the boil. Test a piece of soba—it should be tender to the bite, cooked through but not at all mushy. Drain and rinse under cold water until the noodles are cold. Toss the sesame seeds through the noodles.
3 To assemble, lay a nori sheet shiny-side down on a bamboo sushi mat or flat surface. Place one-sixth

of the noodles along the bottom end of the nori, leaving a 2 cm (3/4 inch) border at one end. Arrange one-sixth of the cucumber, tuna, ginger and mushrooms along the top of the noodles, in the centre. Roll the mat over to enclose the filling and roll the nori up firmly in a cylinder shape. Trim the ends with a very sharp wet knife, cut the roll in half and each half into three, cleaning the knife between each cut. Repeat with the remaining nori sheets, noodles and filling.

Simmer the mushrooms until the liquid has almost evaporated.

4 To make the dipping sauce, combine the wasabi paste, soy sauce and mirin in a bowl and serve with the rolls.

NUTRITION PER PIECE
Fat 1 g; Protein 3 g; Carbohydrate 5 g; Dietary Fibre 1 g; Cholesterol 2 mg; 160 kJ (40 Cal)

COOK'S FILE
Note: Use dashi granules or powder according to packet instructions, as different brands differ in strength of flavour.

Arrange the cucumber and tuna along the centre of the noodles.

CRISPY CHICKEN AND PORK BALLS

Preparation time: 25 minutes +
    5 minutes soaking
Cooking time: 15 minutes
Makes 24

250 g (9 oz) Hokkien egg noodles,
    cut into 5 cm (2 inch) lengths
2 red Asian shallots
1 small stem lemon grass
    (white part only), finely chopped
4 dried curry leaves
2 cloves garlic, roughly chopped
200 g (7 oz) minced (ground) chicken
200 g (7 oz) minced (ground) pork
1 tablespoon chopped coriander
    (cilantro) leaves
2 teaspoons red curry paste
1 tablespoon fish sauce
1 tablespoon lime juice
peanut oil, to deep-fry
sweet chilli sauce, to serve

1 Place the noodles in a large heatproof bowl, cover with boiling water and soak for 1 minute, or until tender and separated. Drain well, rinse under cold water and drain again. Pat dry with paper towels.
2 Place the red Asian shallots, lemon grass, curry leaves and garlic in a mortar and pestle or small food processor and pound or blend until it forms a smooth paste.
3 Place the minced chicken and pork in a bowl, add the lemon grass paste, chopped coriander, red curry paste, fish sauce and lime juice and mix until well combined. Add the noodles and mix well with your hands until the noodles are evenly distributed throughout. Using a tablespoon of mixture at a time, roll each spoonful into a ball to make 24 in total.
4 Fill a heavy-based saucepan one-third full of peanut oil and heat to 170°C (325°F), or until a cube of bread dropped in the oil browns in 20 seconds. Cook the balls in batches for 3–4 minutes each batch, or until golden and cooked through. Drain on paper towels. Serve hot with the sweet chilli sauce.

NUTRITION PER BALL
Fat 1.5 g; Protein 4.5 g; Carbohydrate 5.5 g; Dietary Fibre 0.5 g; Cholesterol 14 mg; 225 kJ (55 Cal)

COOK'S FILE
Notes: Combine the mixture really well with your hands or it won't hold together well when cooking—the balls should be quite compact with the noodles.

Roll the meat and noodle mixture into balls with your hands.

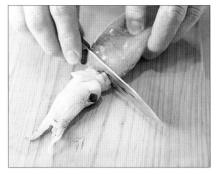

Remove the tentacles and intestines from the squid tube.

Using your fingers, fill each tube with the pork and noodle filling.

BABY SQUID STUFFED WITH PORK AND VERMICELLI NOODLES

Preparation time: 30 minutes +
   10 minutes soaking + cooling
Cooking time: 35 minutes
Serves 6

12 baby squid tubes (about 100 g or
   3½ oz each)
75 g (3 oz) dried rice vermicelli
2 tablespoons peanut oil
2 small red chillies, halved lengthways
   with stem attached
2 cloves garlic, finely chopped
1½ tablespoons grated palm sugar
80 g (½ cup) roughly chopped
   unsalted peanuts
750 g (1 lb 10 oz) minced (ground)
   pork
2 teaspoons yellow bean sauce
   (see Note)
30 g (½ cup) finely chopped Thai basil
25 g (½ cup) finely chopped coriander
   (cilantro) leaves
cornflour (cornstarch), to dust
3 tablespoons oil
lime wedges, to serve

1 To clean the squid, pull out the tentacles and remove the quill from the tube. Pull the skin away from the tubes and discard. Rinse well under cold running water. Pat dry.
2 Place the vermicelli in a large heatproof bowl, cover with boiling water and soak for 6–7 minutes, or until softened. Drain and rinse under cold water. Cut into short lengths.
3 Heat the peanut oil and chilli in a wok over low heat for 2 minutes to infuse. Remove the chilli and increase the heat to high. Add the garlic, palm sugar and peanuts and stir-fry for 5 seconds. Add the mince and stir for 6–7 minutes, or until cooked through, stirring to break up any lumps. Stir in the vermicelli until well combined. Remove from the heat and stir in the yellow bean sauce. Allow to cool slightly, then stir in the herbs. Divide the filling into 12 even portions.
4 Fill each squid tube with a portion of the filling, then lightly dust the outside with cornflour.
5 Heat a clean wok over high heat, add the oil and swirl to coat. Cook

Fry the stuffed squid in batches until golden and tender.

the squid in batches, two at a time, and sear for 2 minutes on each side, or until golden and tender. Drain on paper towels and repeat with the remaining squid. Season with salt and serve with lime wedges.

NUTRITION PER SERVE
Fat 26.5 g; Protein 40 g; Carbohydrate 13 g; Dietary Fibre 1.5 g; Cholesterol 207.5 mg; 1880 kJ (450 Cal)

COOK'S FILE
Note: Yellow bean sauce here refers to the Southeast Asian version, which is made from salted and fermented yellow soy beans. It has a runnier consistency and is paler in colour than the Chinese variety.

STEAMED PORK AND PRAWN DUMPLINGS

Preparation time: 25 minutes
Cooking time: 5 minutes
Makes 24

300 g (10½ oz) minced (ground) pork
300 g (10½ oz) minced (ground)
　prawn (shrimp
3 spring onions (scallions), thinly
　sliced
60 g (⅓ cup) chopped water chestnuts
1½ teaspoons finely chopped
　ginger
1 tablespoon light soy sauce
1 teaspoon caster (superfine) sugar
24 won ton wrappers
light soy sauce, extra, to serve
chilli sauce, to serve

1 Place the minced pork and prawn, spring onion, water chestnuts, ginger, soy sauce and sugar in a large non-metallic bowl and combine well.
2 Working with one wrapper at a time, place a heaped tablespoon of the filling in the centre of the wrapper. Bring the sides up around the outside, forming pleats to firmly encase the filling—the top of the dumpling should be exposed. Pinch together to enclose the bottom of the filling, then cover with a damp cloth. Repeat with the remaining wrappers and filling to make 24 in total.
3 Line a large double bamboo steamer with baking paper. Arrange the dumplings on the base so they don't touch one another. Place over a wok or large saucepan of simmering water, making sure the steamer base doesn't touch the water. Cover and steam for 5 minutes, or until cooked through. Serve the dumplings with soy and chilli sauces, for dipping.

NUTRITION PER DUMPLING
Fat 1 g; Protein 6 g; Carbohydrate 5 g;
Dietary Fibre 0.5 g; Cholesterol 27 mg;
230 kJ (55 Cal)

COOK'S FILE
Variation: If desired, these dumplings can be made using only minced pork—just double the amount.

Form pleats around the dumpling to enclose the filling, leaving the top exposed.

NOODLE AND CRAB OMELETTE

Preparation time: 20 minutes +
  5 minutes soaking
Cooking time: 5 minutes
Serves 6

Tamarind dressing
2¹/2 tablespoons white vinegar
2¹/2 tablespoons lime juice
¹/4 teaspoon tamarind purée
2 tablespoons sugar
1 small red chilli, seeded and finely
  chopped

75 g (3 oz) dried mung bean vermicelli
200 g (7 oz) fresh cooked crab meat
3 spring onions (scallions), finely sliced
2 tablespoons finely chopped
  coriander (cilantro) leaves
2 tablespoons shredded Thai basil
8 eggs
2 small red chillies, seeded and finely
  chopped
1¹/2 tablespoons vegetable oil

1 To make the dressing, whisk the white vinegar, lime juice, tamarind purée, sugar and chilli together in a small bowl.

2 Place the noodles in a large heatproof bowl, cover with boiling water and soak for 3–4 minutes. Drain and rinse under cold water. Cut into short lengths and return to the bowl. Add the crab meat, spring onion, coriander and Thai basil and toss until well combined.

3 Whisk the eggs and chilli in a small bowl until well combined. Heat 1 teaspoon of oil in a wok over high heat and swirl to coat. Pour in a sixth of the egg mixture and swirl to about 16 cm (6¹/2 inch) diameter. Take the wok off the heat when the egg has not quite set in the middle. Remove the omelette from the wok with a spatula and lay out flat on a chopping board. Arrange a sixth of the noodle mixture along one end of the omelette, roll up tightly, then wrap in plastic wrap—twist both ends of the plastic wrap for a tight roll. Repeat with the remaining oil, egg mixture and filling, to make six omelettes in total. Rest for 10 minutes.

4 Remove the plastic wrap from the rolls, trim the ends and cut on the diagonal into three or four even slices. Serve immediately with the tamarind dressing.

NUTRITION PER SERVE
Fat 12 g; Protein 14 g; Carbohydrate 13.5 g; Dietary Fibre 1 g; Cholesterol 298 mg; 910 kJ (220 Cal)

Remove the omelette from the wok when it has not quite set in the middle.

Place the noodle filling along one end of the omelette, then roll up tightly.

SALADS

CRAB AND PAPAYA NOODLE SALAD

Preparation time: 20 minutes +
   10 minutes soaking +
   15 minutes refrigeration
Cooking time: Nil
Serves 4

80 g (3 oz) dried rice vermicelli
250 g (9 oz) green papaya
300 g (10½ oz) fresh cooked
   crab meat
2 tablespoons thinly sliced Chinese
   celery or celery
10 g (½ cup) mint
4 tablespoons finely chopped
   Thai basil
2 tablespoons crisp fried shallots
30 g (1½ oz) roasted peanuts,
   crushed

Dressing
2 tablespoons peanut oil
150 ml (5 fl oz) lime juice
1½ tablespoons fish sauce
2 tablespoons sugar
2 small red chillies, seeded
   and finely chopped

1 Place the vermicelli in a heatproof bowl, cover with boiling water and soak for 6–7 minutes, or until tender. Drain well, rinse in cold water and drain again.

2 Meanwhile, peel the green papaya, cut in half lengthways and scoop out the seeds with a spoon. Cut the fruit into julienne strips and place in a non-metallic bowl. Add the crab meat and celery.

3 To make the dressing, whisk together the peanut oil, lime juice, fish sauce, sugar and chopped chillies in a small bowl.

4 Pour the dressing over the crab and papaya mixture and toss well. Add the noodles, mint and Thai basil and toss again, coating well in the dressing. Cover with plastic wrap and refrigerate for 15 minutes to allow the flavours to develop.

5 Sprinkle the salad with the fried shallot flakes and crushed roasted peanuts just before serving.

NUTRITION PER SERVE
Fat 13.5 g; Protein 13.5 g; Carbohydrate 26 g; Dietary Fibre 2 g; Cholesterol 63 mg; 1180 kJ (280 Cal)

Remove the seeds from the fresh chilli with the point of a sharp knife.

Pour the whisked dressing over the crab mixture.

BON BONJI

Preparation time: 20 minutes +
  cooling time + 4 hours refrigeration
Cooking time: 15 minutes
Serves 4

1 chicken breast fillet (250 g or 9 oz)
2 spring onions (scallions), chopped
750 ml (3 cups) chicken stock
200 g (7 oz) mung bean vermicelli
2 Lebanese (short) cucumbers,
  seeded and julienned into 5 cm
  (2 inch) lengths
2 spring onions (scallions), extra, sliced
2 tablespoons toasted sesame seeds

Dressing
2 tablespoons Chinese sesame
  paste
2 tablespoons light soy sauce
1 tablespoon rice vinegar
¼ teaspoon chilli oil
1½ teaspoons sugar

1 Season the chicken breast well
with salt and black pepper. Put the
spring onion on the bottom of a wok
and place the chicken breast on top.
Gently pour in the stock, bring to a
simmer over low heat and cook,
covered, for 10 minutes, or until just
cooked. Remove the chicken and set
aside to cool, reserving the liquid.
2 Place the vermicelli in a heatproof
bowl, cover with boiling water and
soak for 3–4 minutes. Drain and rinse
under cold water.
3 Meanwhile, to make the dressing,
blend the sesame paste, soy sauce,
rice vinegar, chilli oil, sugar and
150 ml (5 fl oz) of the reserved
poaching liquid in a blender
until smooth.
4 Shred the chicken meat. Toss in a
bowl with the cucumber, noodles,
extra spring onion and dressing until
well combined. Cover with a plastic
wrap and refrigerate for 4 hours.

5 To serve, sprinkle the salad with
the toasted sesame seeds.

NUTRITION PER SERVE
Fat 13.5 g; Protein 19.5 g; Carbohydrate
30.5 g; Dietary Fibre 5 g; Cholesterol
41 mg; 1350 kJ (325 Cal)

COOK'S FILE
Note: This recipe can be served as
individual portions in lettuce cups.

*Pour the sesame paste dressing over the
salad ingredients.*

CHILLED SOBA NOODLES WITH DIPPING SAUCE

Preparation time: 10 minutes +
 cooling time
Cooking time: 10 minutes
Serves 4

1 1/2 teaspoons dashi granules
125 ml (1/2 cup) Japanese soy sauce
3 tablespoons mirin
1 teaspoon sugar
1/4 teaspoon finely grated ginger
 (optional)
250 g (9 oz) dried soba noodles
1 spring onion (scallion), very thinly
 sliced
1 teaspoon wasabi paste

1 Place the dashi powder in a saucepan, pour in 625 ml (2 1/2 cups) boiling water and stir until the granules have dissolved. Add the soy sauce, mirin, sugar and ginger and bring to the boil over high heat, stirring until the sugar has dissolved. Remove from the heat and leave for 4–5 minutes to allow the flavours to infuse, then strain through a very fine sieve, discarding the ginger. Allow to cool, then refrigerate until required. Before serving, divide the sauce among four small Asian rice bowls.

2 Bring a large saucepan of water to the boil over medium heat. Add the noodles and stir to separate. Return to the boil, then add 250 ml (1 cup) cold water. Repeat this step three times as the water just comes to the boil. Test a piece of soba—it should be tender to the bite, cooked through but not mushy. If it's not quite done, repeat one more time. Drain and rinse under cold water until the noodles are cold.

3 To serve, pile the noodles on four serving plates, arranging them slightly to one side. On the other side, place a small pile of spring onion and a little ball of wasabi— these are condiments for the dipping sauce which should be served alongside the noodles.

4 The noodles should be eaten with chopsticks, which are used to mix a little of the spring onion and wasabi into the sauce to taste, then dip small amounts of noodles into the sauce. Don't release the noodles into the sauce, simply dip in with the chopsticks and bring straight to your mouth.

NUTRITION PER SERVE
Fat 0.5 g; Protein 11 g; Carbohydrate 50 g; Dietary Fibre 1.5 g; Cholesterol 0.5 mg; 1025 kJ (245 Cal)

COOK'S FILE
Note: In summer, keep the noodles refreshingly chilled by serving in a bowl, nestled inside a larger bowl of ice.

PORK NOODLE SALAD

Preparation time: 20 minutes +
  10 minutes soaking
Cooking time: 35 minutes
Serves 4–6

Asian broth

250 ml (1 cup) chicken stock
3 coriander (cilantro) roots
2 makrut (kaffir) lime leaves
3 cm x 3 cm (1¼ inch x 1¼ inch)
  piece ginger, sliced

30 g (1 oz) fresh black fungus
100 g (3½ oz) dried rice vermicelli
1 small red chilli, seeded and finely sliced
2 red Asian shallots, thinly sliced
2 spring onions (scallions), thinly sliced
2 cloves garlic, crushed
250 g (9 oz) minced (ground) pork
3 tablespoons lime juice
3 tablespoons fish sauce
1½ tablespoons grated palm sugar
¼ teaspoon ground white pepper
15 g (½ cup) coriander (cilantro)
  leaves, chopped
oakleaf or coral lettuce, to serve
lime wedges, to garnish
long red chilli, seeded and cut into
  strips, to garnish

coriander (cilantro) leaves, extra,
  to garnish (optional)

1 To make the Asian broth, place the stock, coriander roots, lime leaves, ginger and 250 ml (1 cup) water in a saucepan. Simmer for 25 minutes, or until liquid has reduced to 185 ml (¾ cup). Strain and return to the pan.
2 Discard the woody stems from the fungus, then thinly slice. Soak the vermicelli in boiling water for 6–7 minutes. Drain, then cut into 3 cm (1¼ inch) lengths. Combine the vermicelli, fungus, chilli, red Asian shallots, spring onion and garlic.
3 Return the stock to the heat and bring to the boil. Add the minced

pork and stir, breaking up any lumps, for 1–2 minutes, or until the pork changes colour and is cooked. Drain, then add to the vermicelli mixture.
4 Combine the lime juice, fish sauce, palm sugar and white pepper, stirring until the sugar has dissolved. Add to the pork mixture with the coriander and mix well. Season with salt.
5 To assemble, tear or shred the lettuce, then arrange on a serving dish. Spoon on the pork and noodle mixture and garnish with the lime wedges, chilli and extra coriander.

NUTRITION PER SERVE (6)
Fat 3.5 g; Protein 11 g; Carbohydrate 15.5 g; Dietary Fibre 1.5 g; Cholesterol 26.5 mg; 580 kJ (140 Cal)

Cut, then discard the woody ends from the fresh black fungus.

Add the cooked minced pork to the noodles and salad ingredients.

SESAME TUNA AND EGG NOODLE SALAD

Preparation time: 20 minutes
Cooking time: 5 minutes
Serves 4

300 g (10½ oz) fresh flat egg noodles
100 g (3½ oz) watercress, trimmed
2 small Lebanese (short) cucumbers, halved lengthways, thinly sliced
1 small red capsicum (pepper), seeded and thinly sliced
10 g (⅓ cup) coriander (cilantro) leaves
40 g (¼ cup) sesame seeds
40 g (¼ cup) black sesame seeds
3 tuna steaks (about 550 g or 1 lb 4 oz)
peanut oil, to shallow-fry

Dressing

60 ml (¼ cup) kecap manis
1½ tablespoons Chinese rice wine

1 Cook the noodles in a large saucepan of boiling water for 1 minute, or until tender. Drain and rinse under cold water, then drain again. Place in a large bowl with the watercress, cucumber, capsicum and coriander and toss together well.
2 To make the dressing, combine the kecap manis and Chinese rice wine in a small bowl. Pour over the noodle mixture and toss together until well combined.
3 Mix the sesame seeds together on a sheet of baking paper. Pat the tuna steaks dry with paper towel, then coat in the sesame seeds.
4 Fill a large frying pan to 1.5 cm (⅝ inch) with peanut oil and heat to 180°C (350°F), or until a cube of bread dropped into the oil browns in 15 seconds. Fry the tuna steaks for 1–2 minutes on each side—they should still be pink in the centre.

Drain on paper towels, then cut into 1.5 cm (⅝ inch) thick slices across the grain using a very sharp knife.
5 To serve, divide the noodle salad among four serving bowls and arrange strips of tuna on top. Season with salt and freshly ground black pepper and serve immediately.

NUTRITION PER SERVE
Fat 24.5 g; Protein 47.5 g; Carbohydrate 41.5 g; Dietary Fibre 5 g; Cholesterol 59 mg; 2460 kJ (590 Cal)

COOK'S FILE
Note: Slice the tuna immediately after cooking or it will continue to cook through and won't be rare in the centre.

CHILLI SALT SQUID AND CELLOPHANE NOODLE SALAD

Preparation time: 30 minutes +
    30 minutes soaking +
    15 minutes refrigeration
Cooking time: 10 minutes
Serves 4

Dressing

1 tablespoon dried shrimp
2 tablespoons Chinese rice wine
2 tablespoons light soy sauce
1 tablespoon Chinese black vinegar
1 teaspoon chilli garlic sauce
2 teaspoons finely chopped ginger
2 spring onions (scallions), thinly
    sliced
1 teaspoon sesame oil

600 g (1lb 5 oz) cleaned squid tubes
125 ml ($^{1}/_{2}$ cup) lemon juice
250 g (9 oz) dried mung bean
    vermicelli
1 small Lebanese (short) cucumber,
    seeded and cut into batons
90 g (3$^{1}/_{4}$ oz) bean sprouts, trimmed
2 tablespoons chopped coriander
    (cilantro) leaves
1 tablespoon Sichuan peppercorns,
    dry roasted
$^{1}/_{4}$ teaspoon dried chilli flakes
2 teaspoons sea salt
1 teaspoon ground white pepper
1 teaspoon ground black pepper
45 g ($^{1}/_{4}$ cup) rice flour
60 g ($^{1}/_{2}$ cup) plain (all-purpose) flour
peanut oil, to deep-fry
2 egg whites, lightly beaten
coriander (cilantro) leaves, to garnish

1 To make the dressing, place the dried shrimp in a small heatproof bowl, cover with boiling water and soak for 10 minutes. Drain and finely chop. Return the shrimp to the bowl, cover with the rice wine and allow to soak for a further 15 minutes. In a separate bowl, combine the soy sauce, black vinegar, chilli sauce, ginger, spring onion and sesame oil. Set aside.

2 Meanwhile, open out the squid tubes, wash and thoroughly pat dry with paper towels. With the soft inside facing upwards, score a diamond pattern using a small sharp knife, taking care not to cut through all the way. Cut the squid into 4 cm x 2.5 cm (1$^{1}/_{2}$ inch x 1 inch) pieces, place in a flat non-metallic dish and pour the lemon juice on top. Cover with plastic wrap and marinate in the refrigerator for 15 minutes.

3 Place the noodles in a large heatproof dish, cover with boiling water and soak for 3–4 minutes, or until softened. Drain and rinse under cold running water. Drain again, then transfer to a serving bowl. Add the cucumber, bean sprouts and chopped coriander leaves.

4 Combine the dry-roasted Sichuan peppercorns, chilli flakes, sea salt, white pepper and black pepper in a mortar and pestle or spice grinder and grind to a fine powder. Transfer to a bowl with the rice and plain flours and combine thoroughly. Drain the squid and pat dry with paper towels.

5 Fill a deep heavy-based saucepan, wok or deep-fryer one-third full of oil and heat to 180°C (350°F), or until a cube of bread browns in 15 seconds. Dip the squid pieces in the egg white, then coat well in the seasoned flour. Deep-fry in batches of 5 or 6 for about 1 minute, or until lightly golden and cooked through—do not overcrowd the pan. Drain on crumpled paper towels and season to taste with salt and freshly ground black pepper.

6 To serve, add the dressing and shrimp mixture to the noodles and gently toss to combine in a large bowl. Place the squid on top of the noodles, garnish with the coriander leaves and serve immediately.

NUTRITION PER SERVE
Fat 9.5 g; Protein 32.5 g; Carbohydrate 55.5 g; Dietary Fibre 4 g; Cholesterol 298.5 mg; 1900 kJ (455 Cal)

Once the dried shrimp have been soaked, finely chop with a sharp knife.

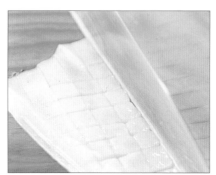

Score a diamond pattern onto the surface of the squid—do not cut all the way through.

Deep-fry the squid pieces until lightly golden and cooked through.

CHINESE CHICKEN AND SESAME NOODLE SALAD

Preparation time: 25 minutes +
  5 minutes soaking +
  1 hour standing
Cooking time: 20 minutes
Serves 4

3 chicken breast fillets
4 slices ginger, 1 cm (1/2 inch) thick
2 tablespoons soy sauce
200 g (7 oz) mung bean vermicelli
2 teaspoons sesame oil
150 g (5 1/2 oz) snow peas
  (mangetout), trimmed
2 spring onions (scallions), thinly sliced
1 teaspoon sesame seeds, toasted

Sesame dressing
1 tablespoon Chinese sesame paste
1 tablespoon chilli bean sauce
2 tablespoons peanut oil
1 tablespoon sugar
1 tablespoon light soy sauce
1 tablespoon Chinese black vinegar
2 tablespoons chicken stock
1 teaspoon sesame oil

1 Put the chicken breasts in a large saucepan with the ginger, soy sauce and 750 ml (3 cups) cold water. Bring to the boil over high heat. Reduce the heat to medium and simmer, covered, for 10 minutes. Remove the pan from the heat and allow to cool in the pan, covered, for 1 hour.

2 Place the vermicelli in a heatproof bowl, cover with boiling water and soak for 3–4 minutes. Drain, then cut into short lengths. Sprinkle with 1 teaspoon of the sesame oil and set aside. Bring a saucepan of water to the boil over high heat. Cook the snow peas for 1 minute. Drain and plunge into a bowl of chilled water. Drain again, then cut in half on the diagonal.

3 To make the dressing, combine the sesame paste, chilli bean sauce, peanut oil, sugar, light soy sauce, black vinegar, chicken stock and the sesame oil in a small bowl.

4 Drain the chicken from the poaching liquid, transfer to a plate and brush lightly with the remaining sesame oil. Shred the chicken finely with a fork, tearing down the grain until you have thin shreds.

5 Place the noodles, half the shredded chicken and a little dressing in a large bowl and toss with the snow peas and spring onion. Arrange on a platter, top with the remaining chicken and dressing and sprinkle with the sesame seeds.

NUTRITION PER SERVE
Fat 24 g; Protein 35 g; Carbohydrate 33 g; Dietary Fibre 4 g; Cholesterol 99 mg; 2050 kJ (490 Cal)

Using a fork, finely shred the poached chicken into small pieces.

SPICY LAMB AND NOODLE SALAD

Preparation time: 15 minutes +
   30 minutes marinating +
   5 minutes standing
Cooking time: 10 minutes
Serves 4

1 tablespoon five-spice powder
3 tablespoons vegetable oil
2 cloves garlic, crushed
2 lamb backstraps (about 250 g or
   9 oz each)
500 g (1 lb 2 oz) fresh Shanghai
   noodles
1½ teaspoons sesame oil
80 g (2¾ oz) snow pea (mangetout)
   sprouts
½ red capsicum (pepper), thinly
   sliced

4 spring onions (scallions), thinly
   sliced on the diagonal
2 tablespoons sesame seeds, toasted

Dressing

1 tablespoon finely chopped
   ginger
1 tablespoon Chinese black vinegar
1 tablespoon Chinese rice wine
2 tablespoons peanut oil
2 teaspoons chilli oil

1 Combine the five-spice powder,
2 tablespoons of the vegetable oil and
garlic in a large non-metallic bowl.
Add the lamb and turn to coat well.
Cover and marinate for 30 minutes.
2 Cook the noodles in a large
saucepan of boiling water for
4–5 minutes, or until tender. Drain,
rinse with cold water and drain

again. Add the sesame oil and toss to
combine thoroughly.
3 Heat the remaining vegetable oil
in a large frying pan. Cook the lamb
over medium–high heat for 3 minutes
each side for medium–rare, or until
cooked to your liking. Rest for
5 minutes, then thinly slice across
the grain.
4 To make the dressing, combine all
the ingredients together.
5 Place the noodles, lamb strips,
snow pea sprouts, capsicum, spring
onion and the dressing in a large
bowl and toss gently until well
combined. Sprinkle with the sesame
seeds and serve immediately.

NUTRITION PER SERVE
Fat 37 g; Protein 38 g; Carbohydrate
64.5 g; Dietary Fibre 4 g; Cholesterol
93 mg; 3140 kJ (750 Cal)

GINGER NOODLE SALAD WITH SALMON, AVOCADO AND PONZU DRESSING

Preparation time: 25 minutes
Cooking time: 20 minutes
Serves 4

500 g (1 lb 2 oz) salmon fillet, skin removed
1 tablespoon oil
1 avocado, halved and stone removed
500 g (1 lb 2 oz) dried soba noodles
3 tablespoons pickled ginger, well drained and shredded
80 g (2¾ oz) mizuna, trimmed
80 ml (⅓ cup) prepared ponzu sauce or 60 ml (¼ cup) soy sauce combined with 1 tablespoon lemon juice
1 tablespoon black sesame seeds

1 Place the salmon in a bowl and rub the surface with the oil, salt and pepper. Slice each avocado half lengthways into quarters, then cut each quarter into 1 cm (½ inch) long pieces from the base to the stem end.

2 Heat a large frying pan over medium–high heat, and just before the pan begins to smoke add the salmon—if your fillet is too large to fit, cut it in half. Cook for 3 minutes on each side, or until golden—this will depend on the size and thickness of your fillet. Remove from the pan and allow to cool.

3 Bring a large saucepan of water to the boil over high heat. Add the noodles and stir to separate. Return to the boil, then add 250 ml (1 cup) cold water. Repeat this step 3 times as the water just comes to the boil. Test a piece of soba—it should be tender to the bite, cooked through but not mushy. If it's not quite done, repeat one more time. Drain and rinse under cold water until the noodles are cold.

4 Combine the noodles, avocado, ginger and mizuna in a large bowl.

Flake the salmon into small pieces with a fork or your fingers and add to the noodles with any juices, then add the ponzu sauce. Gently toss until well combined.

5 To serve, divide the noodle salad among the serving dishes and sprinkle with the sesame seeds.

NUTRITION PER SERVE
Fat 29.5 g; Protein 46 g; Carbohydrate 95.5 g; Dietary Fibre 4 g; Cholesterol 65 mg; 3345 kJ (800 Cal)

Use a fork to flake the salmon fillet into small pieces.

BEEF AND GLASS NOODLE SALAD

Preparation time: 25 minutes +
 5 minutes soaking
Cooking time: 10 minutes
Serves 4

500 g (1 lb 2 oz) beef fillet, 5 cm
 (2 inch) in diameter
1¹/2 tablespoons vegetable oil
1 teaspoon dried shrimp
1 teaspoon jasmine rice
1 stem lemon grass (white part only),
 finely chopped
1 small red chilli, seeded and finely
 chopped
2 coriander (cilantro) roots, finely chopped
2 makrut (kaffir) lime leaves, finely
 shredded
1–2 tablespoons lime juice
2 teaspoons finely chopped ginger
300 g (10¹/2 oz) mung bean vermicelli
1 small Lebanese (short) cucumber,
 peeled, cut in half lengthways and
 cut into 1 cm (¹/2 inch) pieces
1 vine-ripened tomato, cut into 1 cm
 (¹/2 inch) wedges
1 red onion, cut into thin wedges
3 tablespoons Thai basil, torn
3 tablespoons Vietnamese mint
1 tablespoon crisp fried shallots
2 tablespoons coriander (cilantro) leaves

Dressing

80 ml (¹/3 cup) lime juice
2 tablespoons grated palm sugar
1 tablespoon fish sauce
1 small red chilli, seeded and finely
 chopped
1 teaspoon sesame oil
¹/2 teaspoon tamarind purée

1 Heat a chargrill plate or frying pan over high heat. Brush the beef with the oil and season generously with salt and black pepper. Sear on all sides for 3–4 minutes ensuring the meat remains rare in the centre. Remove and allow to rest.
2 Meanwhile, dry-fry the dried shrimp and rice in a clean frying pan for 1–2 minutes, or until fragrant. Place in a spice grinder or mortar and pestle and grind to a fine powder. Mix the powder with the lemon grass, chilli, coriander roots, lime leaves, lime juice and ginger in a non-metallic bowl. Add the beef and turn to coat well on all sides. Cover and marinate for 5 minutes. Cut into 1 cm (¹/2 inch) thick slices across the grain.
3 To make the dressing, combine all the ingredients in a small bowl.
4 Place the vermicelli in a heatproof bowl, cover with boiling water and soak for 3–4 minutes, or until softened. Drain, rinse under cold water and drain again. Transfer the noodles to a large bowl, then add the beef, cucumber, tomato, red onion, basil, mint and dressing and toss well. Serve garnished with the crisp fried shallots and coriander leaves.

NUTRITION PER SERVE
Fat 12 g; Protein 28.5g; Carbohydrate 48.5 g; Dietary Fibre 4 g; Cholesterol 84 mg; 1765 kJ (420 Cal)

Add the beef to the marinade, then turn to coat well on all sides.

COLD SICHUAN NOODLES WITH WHITE-CUT CHICKEN

Preparation time: 15 minutes + cooling time
Cooking time: 15 minutes
Serves 4

5 cm x 5 cm (2 inch x 2 inch) piece ginger, sliced
1/2 teaspoon black peppercorns
2 tablespoons celery leaves
8 spring onions (scallions), thinly sliced
3 chicken breast fillets (about 200 g or 7 oz each)
1 teaspoon Sichuan peppercorns
500 g (1 lb 2 oz) dried somen noodles
3 tablespoons crisp fried garlic flakes
40 g (1 1/2 oz) shredded Chinese broccoli (gai lan) leaves
2 small Lebanese (short) cucumbers, cut into batons

Dressing
1/2 teaspoon sesame oil
80 ml (1/3 cup) light soy sauce
1 tablespoon Chinese black vinegar
2 teaspoons Chinese rice wine

1 Place the ginger, peppercorns, celery leaves, half the spring onion, 1 teaspoon salt and the chicken in a large saucepan. Add enough cold water to cover and bring to the boil over high heat. Reduce the heat to medium, cover and simmer for 10 minutes, or until cooked through. Remove the chicken, cool slightly and cut into 1.5 cm (5/8 inch) slices on the diagonal.

2 Meanwhile, dry-fry the Sichuan peppercorns in a frying pan for 1 minute, or until the peppercorns are dark and aromatic. Place in a spice grinder or mortar and pestle and grind to a fine powder.

3 To make the dressing, whisk the sesame oil, light soy sauce, black vinegar and Chinese rice wine until well combined.

4 Cook the noodles in a large saucepan of boiling water for 2 minutes, or until tender. Drain and rinse under cold water, then drain again. Transfer to a large bowl and add the chicken, crisp fried garlic flakes, Chinese broccoli leaves, cucumber, ground Sichuan pepper, the dressing and the remaining spring onion and toss until well combined. Season to taste with salt and freshly ground black pepper and serve.

NUTRITION PER SERVE
Fat 9.5 g; Protein 39 g; Carbohydrate 33.5 g; Dietary Fibre 3.5 g; Cholesterol 99 mg; 1595 kJ (380 Cal)

Dry-fry the peppercorns in a clean frying pan until they darken.

SPICY FUN SEE NOODLE SALAD

Preparation time: 20 minutes +
    5 minutes soaking +
    2 hours refrigeration
Cooking time: 5 minutes
Serves 4

125 g (4½ oz) mung bean vermicelli
1 teaspoon sesame oil
1 large carrot, julienned
2 sticks celery, julienned
100 g (3½ oz) snow peas
    (mangetout), julienned
2 small Lebanese (short) cucumbers,
    seeded and julienned
3 spring onions (scallions), thinly
    sliced into long diagonal strips
15 g (½ cup) coriander (cilantro) leaves
10 g (½ cup) mint

Dressing
70 g (⅓ cup) Chinese sesame paste
2 teaspoons chilli oil

60 ml (¼ cup) light soy sauce
1 tablespoon white vinegar
1 tablespoon sugar
¼ teaspoon cayenne pepper
2½ tablespoons chicken stock

1 Place the noodles in a large heatproof bowl, cover with boiling water and soak for 3–4 minutes, or until softened. Drain. Cut in half with scissors, place in a large bowl, add the sesame oil and mix well. Cover and refrigerate for 1 hour, or until needed.
2 Bring a saucepan of water to the boil, add the carrot, celery, snow peas and 2 teaspoons salt and cook for 30 seconds. Drain and refresh in icy cold water. Drain again and pat dry, making sure all the water is drained—squeeze out in a clean tea towel, if necessary. Combine with the cucumber and spring onion and refrigerate for 1 hour.
3 To make the dressing, place the

sesame paste in a bowl and stir well. Slowly mix in the chilli oil, soy sauce, vinegar, sugar, cayenne pepper and chicken stock.
4 Just before serving, add three-quarters of the blanched vegetables and three-quarters of the herbs to the chilled noodles. Pour the dressing on top, then toss well. Season to taste with salt and pepper. Transfer to a serving platter and top with the remaining vegetables and herbs.

NUTRITION PER SERVE
Fat 13 g; Protein 6 g; Carbohydrate 25.5 g; Dietary Fibre 6.5 g; Cholesterol 0 mg; 1020 kJ (245 Cal)

COOK'S FILE
Note: To make this a purely vegetarian dish, vegetable stock can be used instead of the chicken stock in the dressing.

PRAWN AND MANGO NOODLE SALAD

Preparation time: 25 minutes +
  5 minutes soaking + chilling time
Cooking time: Nil
Serves 4–6

Dressing
1 1/2 tablespoons fish sauce
2 tablespoons lime juice
2 teaspoons soft brown sugar
1 tablespoon sweet chilli sauce
2 teaspoons light soy sauce
1 small red chilli, seeded and finely
  sliced

150 g (5 1/2 oz) mung bean vermicelli
2 teaspoons peanut oil
1 large ripe mango (470 g or 1 lb 1 oz)
700 g (1 lb 9 oz) cooked medium prawns
  (shrimp), peeled and deveined,
  well chilled

1/2 red onion, thinly sliced
25 g (1/2 cup) chopped coriander
  (cilantro) leaves
20 g (1/3 cup) chopped Vietnamese
  mint
50 g (1 3/4 oz) mizuna
2 tablespoons chopped roasted
  peanuts

1 To make the dressing, combine the fish sauce, lime juice, brown sugar, sweet chilli sauce, soy sauce and chilli in a small bowl and stir until the sugar has dissolved.
2 Place the noodles in a large heatproof bowl, cover with boiling water and soak for 3–4 minutes, or until softened. Drain and rinse under cold water. Cut into 10 cm (4 inch) lengths with scissors. Transfer to a large bowl, add the peanut oil and toss together well.

3 Peel the mango and cut into thin strips, about 3 mm (1/8 inch) wide. Add to the noodles with the prawns, red onion, coriander leaves and mint. Pour the dressing on the salad and toss gently, taking care not to break up the mango slices or noodles.
4 To serve, arrange the mizuna on a large serving plate, spoon the salad on top and garnish with the chopped peanuts. Serve chilled.

NUTRITION PER SERVE (6)
Fat 4.5 g; Protein 26.5 g; Carbohydrate 20.5 g; Dietary Fibre 2.5 g; Cholesterol 174 mg; 956 kJ (230 Cal)

COOK'S FILE
Hint: Wear rubber gloves when working with chillies. And remember, the smaller the chilli the more intense the heat.

CHINESE ROAST DUCK, LIME, HERB AND NOODLE SALAD

Preparation time: 25 minutes +
20 minutes soaking
Cooking time: 10 minutes
Serves 4

Dressing
60 ml (¼ cup) fish sauce
2 tablespoons lime juice
1 tablespoon grated palm sugar
1 small red chilli, finely chopped

250 g (9 oz) dried flat rice stick
noodles (5 mm or ¼ inch thick)
1 Chinese roast duck
1 tablespoon julienned ginger

90 g (3¼ oz) bean sprouts
1 small red onion, thinly sliced
3 tablespoons coriander (cilantro)
leaves
3 tablespoons Thai basil or basil
1 lime, quartered

1 To make the dressing, combine the fish sauce, lime juice, palm sugar and chilli in a small bowl.
2 Place the noodles in a large bowl, cover with warm water and soak for 15–20 minutes, or until *al dente*. Drain, then return to the bowl.
3 Preheat the oven to moderate 180°C (350°F/Gas 4). Remove the flesh and skin from the duck in large pieces, then cut into thin strips. Place on a baking tray and heat in the oven for 10 minutes, or until the duck is warmed through.
4 Add the ginger, bean sprouts, onion, coriander, basil and the dressing to the noodles and toss until well combined. Serve the salad on a platter, or on individual serving plates or bowls, and arrange the duck strips on top. Serve with lime wedges.

NUTRITION PER SERVE
Fat 25.5 g; Protein 24.5 g; Carbohydrate 45.5 g; Dietary Fibre 2.5 g; Cholesterol 115.5 mg; 2130 kJ (510 Cal)

COOK'S FILE
Note: For crispy-skinned duck, place under a hot grill for 1 minute, or until crisp. Arrange on the salad and serve immediately.

SOMEN NOODLE SALAD WITH SESAME DRESSING

Preparation time: 25 minutes + cooling time
Cooking time: 5 minutes
Serves 4

Sesame dressing
40 g (1/3 cup) sesame seeds, toasted
2 1/2 tablespoons Japanese or light soy sauce
2 tablespoons rice vinegar
2 teaspoons sugar
1/2 teaspoon grated ginger
1/2 teaspoon dashi granules

125 g (4 1/2 oz) dried somen noodles
100 g (3 1/2 oz) snow peas (mangetout), finely sliced on the diagonal
100 g (3 1/2 oz) daikon radish, julienned
1 small (100 g or 3 1/2 oz) carrot, julienned
1 spring onion (scallion), sliced on the diagonal

50 g (1 3/4 oz) baby English spinach leaves, trimmed
2 teaspoons toasted sesame seeds

1 To make the dressing, place the sesame seeds in a mortar and pestle and grind until fine and moist. Combine the soy sauce, rice vinegar, sugar, ginger, dashi granules and 125 ml (1/2 cup) water in a small saucepan and bring to the boil over high heat. Reduce the heat to medium and simmer, stirring, for 2 minutes, or until the dashi granules have dissolved. Remove from the heat. Cool. Gradually combine with the ground sesame seeds, stirring to form a thick dressing.

2 Cook the noodles in a large saucepan of boiling water for 2 minutes, or until tender. Drain the noodles then, rinse under cold water and cool completely. Cut into 10 cm (4 inch) lengths using scissors.

3 Place the snow peas in a large shallow bowl with the daikon, carrot, spring onion, English spinach leaves and the noodles. Add the dressing and toss well to combine. Place in the refrigerator until ready to serve. Just before serving, sprinkle the top with the toasted sesame seeds.

NUTRITION PER SERVE
Fat 7.5 g; Protein 8 g; Carbohydrate 27 g; Dietary Fibre 4 g; Cholesterol 0.5 mg; 885 kJ (210 Cal)

Pour the soy sauce mixture into the sesame seeds, stirring to form a thick dressing.

SOY CHICKEN AND GREEN TEA NOODLE SALAD

Preparation time: 30 minutes +
cooling time + 2 hours marinating
Cooking time: 20 minutes
Serves 4–6

200 g (7 oz) dried green tea soba
noodles
2 1/2 teaspoons sesame oil
2 chicken breast fillets (about 200 g
or 7 oz each)
3 teaspoons grated ginger
80 ml (1/3 cup) Japanese soy sauce
60 ml (1/4 cup) mirin
1 1/2 tablespoons sake
3/4 teaspoon dashi granules
3/4 teaspoon sugar
3 teaspoons rice vinegar
1 small Lebanese (short) cucumber, cut
in half lengthways and thinly sliced
1 tablespoon pickled ginger, shredded
2 spring onions (scallions), sliced on
the diagonal
1 tablespoon black sesame seeds

1 Bring a large saucepan of water to the boil over high heat. Add the noodles and stir to separate. Return to the boil, then add 250 ml (1 cup) cold water. Repeat this step three times as the water just comes to the boil. Test a piece of soba—it should be tender to the bite, cooked through but not mushy. If it's not quite done, repeat one more time. Drain and rinse under cold water until the noodles are cold. Cut into 10 cm (4 inch) lengths using scissors. Toss with 2 teaspoons of the sesame oil.
2 Place the chicken in a non-metallic bowl. Combine the ginger, soy sauce, mirin, sake and the remaining sesame oil, then pour over the chicken and turn until well coated. Cover and refrigerate for 2 hours.
3 Line a bamboo steamer with baking paper. Remove the chicken, reserving the marinade and place the fillets in the steamer. Place the steamer over a wok or saucepan of simmering water, making sure the base doesn't touch the water. Cover

and steam for 8–10 minutes, or until cooked through. Remove and allow to cool completely.
4 Place the reserved marinade in a small saucepan with the dashi granules, sugar, rice vinegar and 90 ml (3 fl oz) water. Bring to the boil, then reduce the heat and simmer for 4–5 minutes. Remove and cool completely in the refrigerator.
5 Place the cucumber, pickled ginger, spring onion and noodles in a large bowl. Cut the chicken breasts into 5 mm (1/4 inch) strips on the diagonal. Add to the noodles. Pour on the dressing and toss well. Serve sprinkled with the sesame seeds.

NUTRITION PER SERVE (6)
Fat 6.5 g; Protein 19.5 g; Carbohydrate 25 g; Dietary Fibre 1.5 g; Cholesterol 44 mg; 1040 kJ (250 Cal)

COOK'S FILE
Note: If green tea noodles (cha soba) are not available, plain soba noodles may be used instead. Both are available from Asian supermarkets.

STIR-FRIES

THAI FRIED NOODLES (PHAD THAI)

Preparation time: 40 minutes +
   20 minutes soaking
Cooking time: 10 minutes
Serves 4–6

250 g (9 oz) flat dried rice stick
   noodles
1 tablespoon tamarind purée
1 small red chilli, chopped
2 cloves garlic, chopped
2 spring onions (scallions), sliced
1½ tablespoons sugar
2 tablespoons fish sauce
2 tablespoons lime juice
2 tablespoons oil
2 eggs, beaten
150 g (5½ oz) pork fillet, thinly sliced
8 large prawns (shrimp), peeled,
   deveined and tails intact
100 g (3½ oz) fried tofu puffs,
   julienned
90 g (3¼ oz) bean sprouts
40 g (¼ cup) chopped roasted
   peanuts
3 tablespoons coriander (cilantro)
   leaves
1 lime, cut into wedges

1 Place the noodles in a heatproof bowl, cover with warm water and soak for 15–20 minutes, or until *al dente*. Drain well.

2 Combine the tamarind purée with 1 tablespoon water. Place the chilli, garlic and spring onion in a spice grinder or mortar and pestle and grind to a smooth paste. Transfer the mixture to a bowl and stir in the tamarind mixture along with the sugar, fish sauce and lime juice, stirring until combined.

3 Heat a wok until very hot, add 1 tablespoon of the oil and swirl to coat the side. Add the egg, swirl to coat and cook for 1–2 minutes, or until set. Remove, roll up and cut into thin slices.

4 Heat the remaining oil in the wok, stir in the chilli mixture, and stir-fry for 30 seconds. Add the pork and stir-fry for 2 minutes, or until tender. Add the prawns and stir-fry for a further minute, or until pink and curled.

5 Stir in the noodles, egg, tofu and the bean sprouts, and gently toss together until heated through.

6 Serve immediately topped with the peanuts, coriander and lime wedges.

NUTRITION PER SERVE (6)
Fat 13 g; Protein 19.5 g; Carbohydrate 34 g; Dietary Fibre 2 g; Cholesterol 129 mg; 1385 kJ (330 Cal)

Pour the egg into the wok and swirl to coat the base.

MA PO TOFU WITH NOODLES

Preparation time: 20 minutes + soaking
Cooking time: 10 minutes
Serves 4

450 g (1 lb) silken firm tofu, cut into 2 cm (³/4 inch) cubes
375 g (13 oz) Hokkien egg noodles
2 teaspoons cornflour (cornstarch)
1 tablespoon peanut oil
2 teaspoons finely chopped ginger
2 spring onions (scallions), finely sliced on the diagonal
225 g (8 oz) minced (ground) pork
1½ tablespoons salted black beans, rinsed and roughly chopped
1 tablespoon chilli bean paste
1 tablespoon dark soy sauce

125 ml (½ cup) chicken stock
1 tablespoon Chinese rice wine
2 cloves garlic, finely chopped
ground white pepper, to taste
2 spring onions (scallions) (green part only), extra, finely sliced on the diagonal
½ teaspoon sesame oil

1 Place the tofu on paper towel to drain the excess moisture.
2 Place the noodles in a heatproof bowl, cover with boiling water and soak for 1 minute, or until tender and separated. Drain well, rinse under cold water and drain again. Divide among four serving bowls. Combine the cornflour and 1 tablespoon water in a small bowl.
3 Heat the oil in a wok over high heat. Add the ginger and spring

onion and cook for 30 seconds, then add the minced pork and stir-fry for 2 minutes, or until almost cooked. Add the black beans, chilli bean paste and soy sauce and stir-fry for 1 minute. Stir in the chicken stock, rice wine and tofu and cook for 3 minutes, or until heated through.
4 Stir the cornflour mixture and garlic into the wok and cook for a further minute, or until thickened. Spoon over the noodles and season with ground white pepper. Garnish with the extra spring onion and drizzle with the sesame oil.

NUTRITION PER SERVE
Fat 18 g; Protein 35 g; Carbohydrate 55 g; Dietary Fibre 5 g; Cholesterol 46.5 mg; 2210 kJ (530 Cal)

PANCIT CANTON

Preparation time: 30 minutes
Cooking time: 20 minutes
Serves 4

1¹/₂ tablespoons peanut oil
1 large onion, finely chopped
2 cloves garlic, finely
    chopped
2 cm x 2 cm (³/₄ inch x ³/₄ inch) piece
    ginger, shredded
500 g (1 lb 2 oz) chicken thigh fillets,
    trimmed and cut into 2 cm
    (³/₄ inch) pieces
180 g (4 cups) Chinese cabbage
    (wom bok), shredded
1 carrot, julienned
200 g (7 oz) Chinese barbecued pork
    (char siu), cut into 5 mm (¹/₄ inch)
    thick pieces
3 teaspoons Chinese rice wine
2 teaspoons sugar

150 g (5¹/₂ oz) snow peas
    (mangetout), trimmed
330 ml (1¹/₃ cups) chicken stock
1 tablespoon light soy sauce
227 g (8 oz) pancit canton (or Chinese
    e-fu) noodles (see Note)
1 lemon, cut into wedges

1 Heat a wok over high heat, add
the oil and swirl to coat. Add the
onion and cook for 2 minutes, then
add the garlic and ginger and cook
for a further minute. Add the chicken
and cook for 2–3 minutes, or until
browned. Stir in the cabbage, carrot,
pork, rice wine and sugar and cook
for a further 3–4 minutes, or until
the pork is heated and the vegetables
have softened. Add the snow peas
and cook for 1 minute, or until tender.
Remove the mixture from the wok.
2 Add the stock and soy sauce to
the wok and bring to the boil. Add

the noodles and cook, stirring, for
3–4 minutes, or until soft and almost
cooked through.
3 Return the stir-fry mixture to the
wok and toss with the noodles for
1 minute, or until combined. Divide
among four warmed serving dishes
and garnish with lemon wedges.

NUTRITION PER SERVE
Fat 18.5 g; Protein 48 g; Carbohydrate
38 g; Dietary Fibre 4 g; Cholesterol
180 mg; 2155 kJ (515 Cal)

COOK'S FILE
Note: Pancit canton noodles are
mostly used in China and the
Philippines, where they are called
'birthday' or 'long-life' noodles—their
length denotes a long life for those
who eat them. These round cakes of
pre-boiled, deep-fried noodles are
delicate and break easily. They are
available in Asian grocery stores.

NOODLES WITH BEEF (PHAD SI-IEW)

Preparation time: 20 minutes
Cooking time: 20 minutes
Serves 4–6

500 g (1 lb 2 oz) fresh rice noodle
   sheets
2 tablespoons peanut oil
2 eggs, lightly beaten
500 g (1 lb 2 oz) rump steak, thinly
   sliced across the grain
60 ml (¼ cup) kecap manis
1½ tablespoons soy sauce
1½ tablespoons fish sauce
300 g (10½ oz) Chinese broccoli (gai
   lan), cut into 5 cm (2 inch) lengths
¼ teaspoon ground white pepper
lemon wedges, to serve

1 Cut the noodle sheets lengthways into 2 cm (¾ inch) strips. Cover the strips with boiling water, then gently separate.

2 Heat a wok over medium heat, add 1 tablespoon of the oil and swirl to coat the side. Add the egg, swirl to coat and cook for 1–2 minutes, or until set. Remove, roll up, then cut into shreds.

3 Reheat the wok over high heat, add the remaining oil and swirl to coat. Stir-fry the beef in batches for 3 minutes, or until brown. Remove the beef to a side plate.

4 Reduce the heat to medium, add the noodles and stir-fry for 2 minutes. Combine the kecap manis, soy sauce and fish sauce. Add to the wok with the broccoli and white pepper, then stir-fry for a further 2 minutes. Return the egg and beef to the wok and stir-fry for another 3 minutes, or until the broccoli has wilted and the noodles are soft but not falling apart. Serve with the lemon wedges on the side.

NUTRITION PER SERVE (6)

Fat 12 g; Protein 24 g; Carbohydrate 19 g; Dietary Fibre 1.5 g; Cholesterol 121 mg; 1175 kJ (280 Cal)

COOK'S FILE

Note: Rice noodles should not be refrigerated.

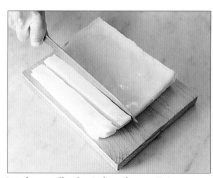

Cut the noodle sheets lengthways into even strips.

POTATO STARCH NOODLE AND VEGETABLE STIR-FRY

Preparation time: 20 minutes +
    10 minutes soaking
Cooking time: 10 minutes
Serves 4

2 tablespoons light soy sauce
1 tablespoon dark soy sauce
1 tablespoon Chinese black vinegar
1 teaspoon sugar
80 ml (1/3 cup) chicken stock
1 tablespoon cornflour (cornstarch)
150 g (5 1/2 oz) dried potato starch
    noodles (Korean vermicelli)
2 tablespoons peanut oil
1 teaspoon sesame oil
1 onion, sliced
4 cloves garlic, finely chopped
1 tablespoon finely chopped ginger
2 small red chillies, seeded and
    chopped
4 spring onions (scallions), finely
    sliced
1 carrot, julienned
1 red capsicum (pepper), julienned

200 g (7 oz) broccoli, cut into small
    florets
115 g (4 oz) baby corn, cut in half
    lengthways
100 g (3 1/2 oz) snow peas (mangetout),
    cut into thirds on the diagonal
300 g (10 1/2 oz) bok choy (pak choi,
    or any Asian green), cut into 10 cm
    (4 inch) lengths
150 g (5 1/2 oz) bean sprouts
3 tablespoons chopped coriander
    (cilantro) leaves

1 Place the light and dark soy sauces, black vinegar, sugar, chicken stock and cornflour in a bowl and stir until the sugar is dissolved.
2 Place the noodles in a large heatproof bowl, cover with boiling water and soak for 10 minutes, or until softened. Drain. Cut in half with scissors, then toss through 1/2 tablespoon of the peanut oil.
3 Heat a large wok over high heat, add the remaining peanut oil and swirl to coat. Add the sesame oil and onion and stir-fry for 2 minutes, or until the onion starts to soften. Add the garlic, ginger, chilli and half the spring onion and stir-fry for 30 seconds. Add the carrot, capsicum, broccoli, corn and snow peas and stir-fry for 2 minutes, or until the vegetables are almost cooked. Add the bok choy and bean sprouts and stir-fry for 1 minute, or until wilted.
4 Add the noodles to the wok with the soy sauce mixture and quickly stir-fry for 1–2 minutes, or until well combined and the sauce thickens. Sprinkle with the coriander and the remaining spring onion and serve.

NUTRITION PER SERVE
Fat 11 g; Protein 13 g; Carbohydrate 41.5 g; Dietary Fibre 9.5 g; Cholesterol 0 mg; 1345 kJ (320 Cal)

COOK'S FILE
Note: The potato starch noodles, sold as 'dung myun', are grey-green in colour and extremely long. Use the noodles that are made in Korea which are quite long and thick.

ANTS CLIMBING TREES (SPICY CELLOPHANE NOODLES WITH MINCED PORK)

Preparation time: 15 minutes +
   15 minutes marinating +
   5 minutes soaking
Cooking time: 15 minutes
Serves 4

200 g (7 oz) minced (ground) pork
1 teaspoon cornflour (cornstarch)
1½ tablespoons light soy sauce
2 tablespoons Chinese rice wine
1 teaspoon sesame oil
150 g (5½ oz) mung bean vermicelli
2 tablespoons oil
4 spring onions (scallions), finely
   chopped
1 clove garlic, crushed
1 tablespoon finely chopped ginger
2 teaspoons chilli bean sauce
185 ml (¾ cup) chicken stock
½ teaspoon sugar
2 spring onions (scallions) (green part
   only), extra, thinly sliced on the
   diagonal

1 Combine the minced pork, cornflour, 1 tablespoon of the soy sauce, 1 tablespoon of the rice wine and ½ teaspoon of the sesame oil in a bowl, using a fork or your fingers. Cover with plastic wrap and marinate for 10–15 minutes.

2 Meanwhile, place the noodles in a heatproof bowl, cover with boiling water and soak for 3–4 minutes, or until softened. Drain well.

3 Heat a wok over high heat, add the oil and swirl to coat. Cook the spring onion, garlic, ginger and chilli bean sauce for 10 seconds, then add the meat mixture and cook for

2 minutes, stirring to break up any lumps. Stir in the stock, sugar, ½ teaspoon salt, and the remaining soy sauce, rice wine and sesame oil.

4 Add the noodles to the wok and toss to combine. Bring to the boil, then reduce the heat to low and simmer, stirring occasionally, for 7–8 minutes, or until the liquid is almost completely absorbed. Garnish with the extra spring onion and serve.

NUTRITION PER SERVE
Fat 13.5 g; Protein 11.5 g; Carbohydrate 23 g; Dietary Fibre 2 g; Cholesterol 30 mg; 1125 kJ (270 Cal)

Add the remaining soy sauce, rice wine and sesame oil to the meat mixture.

Toss the noodles and meat mixture together in the wok until combined.

BEEF KEUH TEOW

Preparation time: 15 minutes
Cooking time: 15 minutes
Serves 4

600 g (1 lb 5 oz) fresh flat rice noodles
   (about 2 cm or ¾ inch wide)
60 ml (¼ cup) peanut oil
150 g (5½ oz) bacon, thinly sliced
300 g (10½ oz) beef round, blade or
   sirloin steak, thinly sliced across
   the grain
3 cloves garlic, crushed
4 small red chillies, seeded and finely
   sliced
12 spring onions (scallions), thinly
   sliced
250 g (9 oz) bean sprouts
3 tablespoons sugar
80 ml (⅓ cup) soy sauce
80 ml (⅓ cup) oyster sauce
3 eggs, lightly beaten
4 spring onions (scallions) (green part
   only), thinly sliced, extra

1 Place the noodles in a heatproof bowl, cover with boiling water and soak briefly. Gently separate the noodles with your hands and drain.
2 Heat a wok over high heat until hot, add 1 tablespoon of the peanut oil and swirl to coat. Add the bacon and stir-fry for 1–2 minutes, or until crispy. Remove from the wok. Heat 1 tablespoon of the oil in the wok, add the beef strips and cook for 1–2 minutes, or until browned. Remove from the wok.
3 Heat the remaining oil in the wok, add the garlic, chilli and spring onion and stir-fry over high heat for 5 seconds. Add the bean sprouts and continue to stir-fry for another 10 seconds, then add the sugar, soy sauce, oyster sauce and noodles and stir-fry for 1–2 minutes, or until the noodles brown slightly. Return the bacon and beef to the wok and toss well for 1–2 minutes to heat through.
4 Push the noodle mixture to one side of the wok, then pour in the egg.

Turn the noodle mixture on top of the egg and let it cook, without stirring, for 5 seconds. Invert the noodles and egg in one turn onto the serving dish so a little of the egg is on top of the noodles. Garnish with the extra sliced spring onion and serve immediately.

NUTRITION PER SERVE
Fat 29 g; Protein 38.5 g; Carbohydrate 83.5 g; Dietary Fibre 5 g; Cholesterol 216.5 mg; 3135 kJ (750 Cal)

Push the noodle mixture to one side of the wok, then pour in the egg.

MUNG BEAN VERMICELLI WITH LAMB AND PEANUTS

Preparation time: 20 minutes +
25 minutes soaking +
1 hour marinating
Cooking time: 15 minutes
Serves 4

6 dried Chinese mushrooms
100 g (3½ oz) mung bean vermicelli
300 g (10½ oz) lamb fillet, thinly
    sliced across the grain
60 ml (¼ cup) soy sauce
2 teaspoons sugar
1½ tablespoons sesame oil
5 cloves garlic, finely chopped
60 ml (¼ cup) peanut oil
2 small red chillies, finely chopped
1 large carrot, julienned
2 small zucchini (courgettes),
    julienned
175 g (6 oz) baby English spinach
    leaves, trimmed
5 spring onions (scallions), thinly
    sliced on the diagonal
50 g (⅓ cup) unsalted peanuts,
    crushed
7 g (¼ cup) coriander (cilantro)
    leaves, chopped
white pepper, to taste

1 Place the Chinese mushrooms in a heatproof bowl, cover with boiling water and soak for 20 minutes, or until softened. Drain and squeeze out the excess water. Discard the woody stems, then thinly slice the caps. Place the noodles in a heatproof bowl, cover with boiling water and soak for 3–4 minutes, or until softened. Drain and cut into 8 cm (3 inch) lengths with scissors.
2 Place the lamb in a non-metallic bowl. Combine the soy sauce, sugar, 1 tablespoon of sesame oil and half the garlic, pour over the lamb and turn until well coated. Cover with plastic wrap and marinate for 1 hour.
3 Heat a large wok over high heat, add 1 tablespoon of the peanut oil and 1 teaspoon of the sesame oil and swirl to coat. Stir-fry the lamb in two batches (adding another 1 tablespoon of the peanut oil and 1 teaspoon of the sesame oil with each batch), for 2 minutes, or until brown. Remove and keep warm.
4 Wipe the wok clean with paper towels, then return to high heat. Add the remaining peanut oil and swirl to coat. Stir-fry the chilli and remaining garlic for 30 seconds. Add the carrot and the zucchini and cook for 2 minutes. Add the spinach, spring onion and mushrooms and cook for 1 minute. Return the lamb and any juices to the wok and stir-fry for 1–2 minutes to heat through. Add the noodles with half the crushed peanuts and coriander, season to taste with white pepper and toss together until well combined. Garnish with the remaining peanuts and coriander.

NUTRITION PER SERVE
Fat 27.5 g; Protein 21.5 g; Carbohydrate 20 g; Dietary Fibre 5 g; Cholesterol 48.5 mg; 1715 kJ (410 Cal)

Return the lamb to the wok with any pan juices.

EGG NOODLES WITH LAP CHEONG

Preparation time: 10 minutes
Cooking time: 15 minutes
Serves 4 (as a side dish)

200 g (7 oz) dried flat egg noodles (5 mm or ¼ inch wide)
5 lap cheong (Chinese pork sausages), (about 150 g or 5½ oz)
2 eggs, lightly beaten
2 teaspoons sesame oil
1 tablespoon peanut oil
2 cloves garlic, crushed
1 tablespoon finely chopped ginger
4 spring onions (scallions), finely chopped
1 spring onion (scallion), extra, thinly sliced on the diagonal
soy sauce, to serve

1 Cook the egg noodles in a large saucepan of boiling water for 3 minutes, or until tender. Drain, rinse and drain again.
2 Place the lap cheong on a small heatproof plate, then in a bamboo steamer and cover. Place over a wok of simmering water (ensure the base doesn't touch the water) and steam for 10 minutes, or until heated through. Remove, reserving the juices left on the plate. Cut the lap cheong into thin slices on the diagonal.
3 Place the egg, sesame oil and ½ teaspoon salt in a small bowl and mix with a fork.
4 Heat a wok until very hot, add the peanut oil and swirl to coat. Cook the garlic and ginger for 30 seconds. Add the noodles and stir-fry for 2–3 minutes, or until heated through.
5 Slowly add the egg mixture, stirring continuously until the egg has just set. Add the lap cheong, any reserved juices and chopped spring onion, and season to taste with salt and ¼ teaspoon freshly ground black pepper. Garnish with the extra spring onion and serve immediately with the soy sauce.

NUTRITION PER SERVE
Fat 19.5 g; Protein 15 g; Carbohydrate 38.5 g; Dietary Fibre 3 g; Cholesterol 130.5 mg; 1615 kJ (385 Cal)

COOK'S FILE
Hint: Place the soy sauce in a little bowl with each serving, for guests to add according to their taste.

Cut the lap cheong evenly into thin slices on the diagonal.

Stir the noodles and the egg mixture until the egg has just set.

CHICKEN, CHILLI JAM AND NOODLE STIR-FRY

Preparation time: 15 minutes +
20 minutes soaking
Cooking time: 10 minutes
Serves 4

250 g (9 oz) flat rice stick noodles
(1 cm or 1/2 inch wide)
400 g (14 oz) chicken breast fillet
1 onion
1 red capsicum (pepper)
1 tablespoon peanut oil
2 tablespoons chilli jam (see Note)
2 teaspoons fish sauce
2 tablespoons light soy sauce
90 g (3 1/4 oz) bean sprouts
100 g (3 1/2 oz) unsalted cashew nuts
30 g (1 cup) loosely packed basil
2 tablespoons basil, extra,
to garnish

1 Place the noodles in a large heatproof bowl, cover with warm water and soak for 15–20 minutes. Drain well.

2 Cut the chicken breast fillets into 5 mm (1/4 inch) slices against the grain. Halve the onion and cut into thin wedges. Cut the capsicum in half, remove the seeds and membrane, then cut into thin strips with a sharp knife.

3 Heat a wok over high heat, add the peanut oil and swirl to coat the side. Cook the onion for 1–2 minutes, or until lightly golden. Add the chicken slices and cook for a further 3–5 minutes, or until browned and almost cooked through. Stir in the chilli jam, then add the capsicum and cook for another minute.

4 Add the fish sauce, soy sauce, bean sprouts, cashew nuts, basil and the noodles to the wok and toss until warmed through and well combined. Garnish with the extra basil and serve immediately.

NUTRITION PER SERVE
Fat 23 g; Protein 30.5 g; Carbohydrate 35 g; Dietary Fibre 4 g; Cholesterol 66 mg; 1960 kJ (470 Cal)

COOK'S FILE
Note: Chilli jam is made with tomato, onion, chilli, oil, tamarind, garlic, sugar, salt, spices and vinegar. It is available in Asian food stores.

CRISPY NOODLES (MEE GROB)

Preparation time: 30 minutes +
    20 minutes soaking
Cooking time: 15 minutes
Serves 4–6

4 dried Chinese mushrooms
oil, to deep-fry
100 g (3½ oz) dried rice vermicelli
100 g (3½ oz) fried tofu, cut into
    matchsticks
4 cloves garlic, crushed
1 onion, chopped
1 chicken breast fillet (about 200 g or
    7 oz), thinly sliced
8 green beans, sliced on the diagonal
6 spring onions (scallions), thinly
    sliced on the diagonal
8 medium prawns (shrimp), peeled,
    deveined and tails intact
30 g (⅓ cup) bean sprouts
coriander (cilantro) leaves, to garnish

Sauce
1 tablespoon light soy sauce
60 ml (¼ cup) white vinegar
5 tablespoons sugar
60 ml (¼ cup) fish sauce
1 tablespoon sweet chilli sauce

1 Soak the mushrooms in boiling water for 20 minutes. Drain, discard the stems and thinly slice the caps.
2 Fill a wok one-third full of oil and heat to 180°C (350°F), or until a cube of bread browns in 15 seconds. Cook the vermicelli in batches for 5 seconds, or until puffed and crispy. Drain on paper towels.
3 Add the tofu to the wok in batches and deep-fry for 1 minute, or until crisp. Drain on paper towels. Cool the oil slightly and carefully remove all but 2 tablespoons of the oil.
4 Reheat the wok until very hot. Add the garlic and onion, and stir-fry for 1 minute. Add the chicken slices, mushrooms, green beans and half the spring onion and stir-fry for 2 minutes, or until the chicken has almost cooked through. Add the prawns and stir-fry for a further 2 minutes, or until the prawns just turn pink.
5 To make the sauce, combine the soy sauce, white vinegar, sugar, fish sauce and sweet chilli sauce. Add to the wok and stir-fry for 2 minutes, or until the meat and prawns are tender and the sauce is syrupy. Remove the wok from the heat and stir in the vermicelli, tofu and bean sprouts. Garnish with the coriander and the remaining spring onion.

NUTRITION PER SERVE (6)
Fat 8.5 g; Protein 14.5 g; Carbohydrate 28.5 g; Dietary Fibre 2 g; Cholesterol 46 mg; 1035 kJ (250 Cal)

Deep-fry the vermicelli in a wok until puffed and crispy.

Stir-fry until the meat and prawns are tender and the sauce is syrupy.

SWEET AND SOUR FISH WITH HOKKIEN NOODLES

Preparation time: 20 minutes
Cooking time: 20 minutes
Serves 4

425 g (15 oz) Hokkien egg noodles
1 tablespoon peanut oil
1 clove garlic, crushed
2 teaspoons grated ginger
1 onion, cut into thin wedges
1 carrot, halved lengthways and thinly sliced
1/2 red capsicum (pepper), cut into thin strips
1/2 green capsicum (pepper), cut into thin strips
1 celery stick, thinly sliced
60 g (1/2 cup) plain (all-purpose) flour
45 g (1/4 cup) rice flour
1 teaspoon caster (superfine) sugar
1/2 teaspoon ground white pepper
500 g (1lb 2 oz) firm white fish fillets (ling, flake, snapper), cut into 3–4 cm (1 1/4 inch–1 1/2) inch cubes
1 egg, beaten with 1 tablespoon water
oil, to deep-fry
2 spring onions (scallions), sliced diagonally

Sauce
60 ml (1/4 cup) rice vinegar
1 tablespoon cornflour (cornstarch)
3 tablespoons tomato sauce
2 tablespoons sugar
2 teaspoons light soy sauce
1 tablespoon dry sherry
60 ml (1/4 cup) pineapple juice
2 tablespoons vegetable stock

1 Soak the noodles in boiling water for 1 minute. Drain.
2 To make the sauce, combine the vinegar and cornflour. Stir in the rest of the ingredients and 185 ml (3/4 cup) water.
3 Heat a wok over medium heat, add the oil and swirl to coat the side. Cook the garlic and ginger for 30 seconds. Add the onion, carrot, red and green capsicum and celery and stir-fry for 3–4 minutes. Add the sauce to the wok, increase the heat to high and stir-fry for 1–2 minutes, or until thickened. Remove from the heat and keep warm.
4 Combine the flours, sugar and white pepper in a bowl. Dip each piece of fish in egg, then coat in the flour mix, shaking off any excess. Fill a deep heavy-based saucepan one-third full of oil and heat to 180°C (350°F), or until a cube of bread browns in 15 seconds. Deep-fry the fish in batches for 3 minutes, or until golden. Drain on paper towels and keep warm.
5 Return the wok with the sauce to medium heat, add the noodles and toss together for 3–4 minutes, or until heated through. Gently toss the fish through, top with the spring onion and serve immediately.

NUTRITION PER SERVE
Fat 10 g; Protein 41.5 g; Carbohydrate 98.5 g; Dietary Fibre 4.5 g; Cholesterol 138 mg; 2760 kJ (660 Cal)

Add the sauce to the wok and stir-fry until the sauce thickens.

PORK AND BROWN BEAN NOODLES

Preparation time: 10 minutes
Cooking time: 20 minutes
Serves 4–6

60 ml (¼ cup) brown bean sauce
2 tablespoons hoisin sauce
185 ml (¾ cup) chicken stock
½ teaspoon sugar
2 tablespoons peanut oil
3 cloves garlic, finely chopped
6 spring onions (scallions), sliced (white and green parts separated)
650 g (1 lb 7 oz) minced (ground) pork
500 g (1 lb 2 oz) Shanghai noodles
1 telegraph (long) cucumber
30 g (1 cup) coriander (cilantro) leaves
90 g (1 cup) bean sprouts
1 tablespoon lime juice

1 Place the brown bean and hoisin sauces, stock and sugar in a bowl and stir until well combined and smooth.
2 Heat a wok over high heat, add the oil and swirl to coat. Add the garlic and the white portion of the spring onion and cook for 10–20 seconds. Add the pork and cook for 2–3 minutes, or until it has changed colour, stirring to break up any lumps. Add the brown bean mixture, reduce the heat to medium and simmer for 7–8 minutes.
3 Cook the noodles in a large saucepan of boiling water for 4–5 minutes, or until tender. Drain and rinse, then divide among individual serving bowls.
4 Cut the cucumber in half lengthways, remove the seeds with a teaspoon and slice on the diagonal. Place in a bowl with the coriander,

bean sprouts, lime juice and the remaining spring onion (green part) and toss together. Spoon the brown sauce over the noodles and top with the cucumber mixture.

NUTRITION PER SERVE (6)
Fat 15 g; Protein 27 g; Carbohydrate 41 g; Dietary Fibre 3 g; Cholesterol 65.5 mg; 1710 kJ (410 Cal)

SINGAPORE NOODLES

Preparation time: 20 minutes +
   20 minutes soaking
Cooking time: 10 minutes
Serves 4

10 g (1/4 oz) dried Chinese mushrooms
375 g (13 oz) thin fresh egg noodles
2 1/2 teaspoons sugar
1 1/2 tablespoons light soy sauce
2 tablespoons Chinese rice wine
1 1/2 tablespoons Madras curry
   powder
150 ml (5 fl oz) coconut milk
125 ml (1/2 cup) chicken stock
2 eggs
1 tablespoon sesame oil
3 tablespoons vegetable oil
2 cloves garlic, finely chopped
1 tablespoon finely chopped ginger
2 small red chillies, seeded and
   finely chopped
3 spring onions (scallions), sliced
300 g (10 1/2 oz) small prawns (shrimp),
   peeled, deveined and cut in half
150 g (5 1/2 oz) Chinese barbecued
   pork (char siu), thinly sliced
120 g (3/4 cup) frozen peas
coriander (cilantro) leaves, to garnish

1 Place the mushrooms in a heatproof bowl, cover with 125 ml (1/2 cup) boiling water and soak for 20 minutes. Drain and reserve the liquid. Discard the stems and finely slice the caps.
2 Meanwhile, cook the noodles in a saucepan of boiling water for 1 minute, then drain and rinse.
3 Combine the reserved mushroom liquid, sugar, soy sauce, rice wine, curry powder, coconut milk and chicken stock in a large bowl. In a separate bowl, lightly beat the eggs and sesame oil together.
4 Heat a wok over high heat, add 2 tablespoons of the vegetable oil and swirl to coat. Cook the garlic, ginger, chilli and mushrooms for 30 seconds. Add the spring onion, prawns, pork, peas and noodles and stir-fry for 2–3 minutes, or until the prawns are cooked and all the ingredients are heated through. Stir in the mushroom liquid mixture until well combined. Pour in the egg

mixture in a thin stream and toss for 1–2 minutes, or until heated through. Serve in deep serving bowls and garnish with coriander leaves.

NUTRITION PER SERVE
Fat 26 g; Protein 43 g; Carbohydrate 59 g; Dietary Fibre 5.5 g; Cholesterol 273 mg; 2715 kJ (650 Cal)

Pour the egg mixture over the noodles in a thin stream.

SQUID WITH CORIANDER, PEPPER AND MUNG BEAN VERMICELLI

Preparation time: 30 minutes +
    5 minutes soaking
Cooking time: 10 minutes
Serves 4

200 g (7 oz) mung bean vermicelli
2 cloves garlic, chopped
2 long red chillies, seeded and
    chopped
25 g (½ cup) chopped coriander
    (cilantro) stems and roots, washed
1 teaspoon black peppercorns,
    dry roasted and crushed
2 tablespoons peanut oil
300 g (10½ oz) cleaned baby squid
    tubes, scored and cut into 3 cm
    (1¼ inch) pieces
100 g (3½ oz) asparagus, stems
    thinly sliced, leaving the tips whole
100 g (3½ oz) sugar snap peas,
    trimmed
2 tablespoons fish sauce
1 tablespoon kecap manis
120 g (¾ cup) roasted unsalted
    peanuts, roughly chopped
    (reserve 2 tablespoons, to garnish)
15 g (½ cup) coriander (cilantro) leaves
1 lime, cut into quarters

1 Put the vermicelli in a heatproof bowl, cover with boiling water and soak for 3–4 minutes, or until softened. Drain, rinse under cold water and drain again. Cut into 15 cm (6 inch) lengths.
2 Place the garlic, chilli, coriander, peppercorns and ½ teaspoon salt in a food processor or blender and process to a rough paste, adding a little water if necessary.
3 Heat the peanut oil in a wok over medium–high heat. Add the paste and cook for 3 minutes, or until fragrant, then push to the side of the wok. Add the squid and briefly stir-fry until it curls, stirring in the paste to coat (it should not be in the wok for more than 1 minute). Remove.
4 Add the asparagus, sugar snap peas and 2 tablespoons water to the wok and stir-fry for 3 minutes, or until the greens are tender. Add the squid and the noodles and toss through to combine. Stir in the fish sauce, kecap manis and peanuts.
5 To serve, divide among four bowls, top with the reserved peanuts and the coriander and serve with lime wedges.

NUTRITION PER SERVE
Fat 23.5 g; Protein 22 g; Carbohydrate 32 g; Dietary Fibre 5.5 g; Cholesterol 149 mg; 1795 kJ (430 Cal)

Stir-fry the squid pieces with the paste until the squid curls.

Toss the squid pieces and the noodles through the greens.

CURRY MEE

Preparation time: 30 minutes +
   30 minutes soaking
Cooking time: 30 minutes
Serves 4

2 long dried red chillies
1 teaspoon shrimp paste
400 g (14 oz) Hokkien egg noodles
1 onion, roughly chopped
4 cloves garlic, roughly chopped
4 stems lemon grass (white part only),
   sliced
1 teaspoon grated ginger
500 ml (2 cups) thick coconut cream
3 tablespoons Malaysian curry
   powder
400 g (14 oz) chicken thigh fillet,
   sliced
120 g (4¼ oz) green beans, trimmed
   and cut into 5 cm (2 inch) lengths
750 ml (3 cups) chicken stock
10 fried tofu puffs, halved diagonally
2 tablespoons fish sauce
2 teaspoons sugar
180 g (2 cups) bean sprouts
2 hard-boiled eggs, quartered
2 tablespoons crisp fried shallots
lime wedges, to serve

1 Soak the chillies in a bowl of water for 30 minutes. Drain and chop. Wrap the shrimp paste in foil and put under a hot grill (broiler) for 1–2 minutes.
2 Place the noodles in a bowl, cover with boiling water and soak for 1 minute to separate. Rinse under cold water, drain and set aside.
3 Place the onion, garlic, lemon grass, ginger, shrimp paste and chilli in a food processor and blend to a rough paste, adding a little water if necessary.
4 Heat 250 ml (1 cup) of the coconut cream in a wok over medium–high heat and simmer for 8–10 minutes, or until it cracks (separates). Stir in the paste and curry powder and cook for 5 minutes, or until fragrant.
5 Add the chicken and beans and cook for 3–4 minutes, or until the chicken is almost cooked. Add the stock, tofu, fish sauce, sugar and the remaining coconut cream and simmer over low heat for 10 minutes, or until the chicken is cooked.

6 Divide the noodles and bean sprouts among four serving bowls and ladle the curry on top. Garnish with the boiled egg quarters and crisp fried shallots. Serve with the lime wedges.

NUTRITION PER SERVE
Fat 39 g; Protein 40.5 g; Carbohydrate 65.5 g; Dietary Fibre 9 g; Cholesterol 209.5 mg; 3230 kJ (670 Cal)

Simmer the coconut cream until it cracks—this is just starting to crack.

Pour the remaining coconut cream into the curry.

PHILIPPINE LONG LIFE NOODLES

Preparation time: 15 minutes +
   20 minutes soaking
Cooking time: 10 minutes
Serves 4

8 dried Chinese mushrooms
400 g (14 oz) pancit canton noodles
   (see Note)
1 tablespoon peanut oil
60 ml (1/4 cup) soy sauce
1 1/2 tablespoons oyster sauce
1 teaspoon sesame oil
1 teaspoon sugar
250 ml (1 cup) chicken stock
2 cloves garlic, crushed
1 tablespoon grated ginger
600 g (1 lb 5 oz) small prawns
   (shrimp), peeled and deveined
4 spring onions (scallions), finely
   chopped on the diagonal

1 Place the mushrooms in a heatproof bowl, cover with boiling water and soak for 20 minutes. Drain. Discard the woody stems and thinly slice the caps.
2 Meanwhile, cook the noodles in a large saucepan of boiling water for 3 minutes. Drain, rinse under cold water, and drain again. Toss with 1 teaspoon of the peanut oil.
3 Combine the soy sauce, oyster sauce, sesame oil, sugar and stock.
4 Heat a wok over high heat, add the remaining peanut oil and swirl to coat. Cook the garlic and ginger for 30 seconds, then add the prawns and stir-fry for 1 minute, or until just cooked through. Add the spring onion, mushrooms and oyster sauce mixture, and bring to the boil for 1 minute. Add the noodles and cook for 2 minutes, or until they have absorbed most of the sauce. Serve.

NUTRITION PER SERVE
Fat 8 g; Protein 42.5 g; Carbohydrate 57.5 g; Dietary Fibre 2.5 g; Cholesterol 236.5 mg; 1990 kJ (475 Cal)

COOK'S FILE
Note: Pancit canton noodles are available in Asian grocery stores. Refer to Note on page 65.

Add the noodles to the wok, separating them with your hands.

79

CHICKEN SATAY NOODLES

Preparation time: 20 minutes +
  5 minutes soaking
Cooking time: 25 minutes
Serves 4

Peanut sauce

1 tablespoon peanut oil
8 red Asian shallots, finely chopped
8 cloves garlic, crushed
1 tablespoon finely chopped ginger
4 small red chillies, finely chopped
250 g (1 cup) crunchy peanut butter
1 1/2 tablespoons light soy sauce
60 ml (1/4 cup) fish sauce
400 ml (14 fl oz) coconut milk
4 tablespoons grated palm sugar
2 makrut (kaffir) lime leaves
80 ml (1/3 cup) lime juice

400 g (14 oz) Hokkien egg noodles
2 tablespoons peanut oil
1 small white onion, finely chopped
2 cloves garlic, finely chopped
1 small red chilli, finely chopped
400 g (14 oz) chicken tenderloins,
  tendon removed, halved
200 g (1 1/4 cups) bean sprouts
150 g (5 1/2 oz) spring onions
  (scallions), chopped

1 small Lebanese (short) cucumber,
  cut in half lengthways and sliced
lime wedges, to serve

1 To make the peanut sauce, heat a wok over medium heat, add the oil and swirl to coat. Add the shallots, garlic, ginger and chilli and cook for 5 minutes. Reduce the heat to low, add the remaining sauce ingredients and simmer for 10 minutes, or until thickened. Remove and keep warm. Discard the lime leaves before serving. If the sauce is too thick, stir in 2 tablespoons water.
2 Place the noodles in a heatproof bowl, cover with boiling water and soak for 1 minute, or until tender and separated. Drain well.

3 Heat a clean wok over high heat, add the oil and swirl to coat. Stir-fry the onion, garlic and chilli for 30 seconds. Add the chicken and cook for 3–4 minutes, or until brown. Stir in the bean sprouts and spring onion and cook for 30 seconds, then add the noodles and toss together for 1–2 minutes, or until heated through.
4 Divide the noodle mixture among the serving bowls and dollop with the peanut sauce. Garnish with the cucumber slices and serve with the lime wedges.

NUTRITION PER SERVE
Fat 83 g; Protein 57 g; Carbohydrate 82 g;
Dietary Fibre 17 g; Cholesterol 103 mg;
5415 kJ (1295 Cal)

Cut the tendon from the chicken tenderloins using a sharp knife.

Remove the lime leaves from the peanut sauce before serving.

Carefully cut the skin from each fish fillet, then discard.

Thoroughly rinse the black beans under cold running water.

WHEAT NOODLES WITH FISH AND BLACK BEANS

Preparation time: 10 minutes
Cooking time: 20 minutes
Serves 4

270 g (9¾ oz) fresh wheat noodles
200 g (7 oz) Chinese broccoli (gai lan), cut into 5 cm (2 inch) lengths
550 g (1 lb 4 oz) snapper or blue-eye cod fillets, skin removed and cut into 4 cm (1½ inch) pieces
2 tablespoons light soy sauce
1½ tablespoons Chinese rice wine
1 teaspoon sugar
½ teaspoon sesame oil
2 teaspoons cornflour (cornstarch)
1 tablespoon vegetable oil
5 cloves garlic, crushed
2 teaspoons finely chopped ginger
2 spring onions (scallions), finely chopped
2 small red chillies, finely chopped
2 tablespoons canned salted black beans, rinsed and roughly chopped
150 ml (5 fl oz) fish stock
spring onions (scallions), extra, sliced on the diagonal, to garnish

1 Cook the wheat noodles in a large saucepan of boiling water for 2 minutes, or until tender. Drain. Place the Chinese broccoli in a steamer and steam for 3–4 minutes, or until slightly wilted. Remove from the heat and keep warm.
2 Place the fish in a bowl. Combine the soy sauce, rice wine, sugar, sesame oil and cornflour. Pour over the fish and toss to coat well.
3 Heat a wok over high heat until very hot, add the vegetable oil and swirl to coat. Add the garlic, ginger, spring onion, chilli and black beans and stir-fry for 1 minute. Add the fish and the marinade and cook for 2 minutes, or until the fish is almost cooked through. Remove the fish with a slotted spoon and keep warm.
4 Add the stock to the wok, reduce the heat to low and bring to a slow simmer. Cook for 5 minutes, or until the sauce has slightly thickened. Return the fish to the wok, cover and continue to simmer gently for 2–3 minutes, or until just cooked.
5 To serve, divide the noodles among the serving dishes, top with the Chinese broccoli and spoon the fish and black bean sauce on top. Garnish with the extra spring onion.

NUTRITION PER SERVE
Fat 8 g; Protein 33 g; Carbohydrate 23.5 g; Dietary Fibre 3.5 g; Cholesterol 84.5 mg; 1280 kJ (305 Cal)

COOK'S FILE
Note: Black beans are fermented and heavily salted black soy beans and are available canned or in packets. Rinse thoroughly before use and, once opened, store in an airtight container in the refrigerator.

YAKISOBA

Preparation time: 30 minutes +
  25 minutes soaking
Cooking time: 10 minutes
Serves 4

4 dried Chinese mushrooms
300 g (10½ oz) fillet steak, thinly
  sliced across the grain
2 large cloves garlic, finely chopped
3 teaspoons finely chopped ginger
500 g (1 lb 2 oz) Hokkien egg noodles
6 rashers streaky bacon, cut into
  3 cm (1¼ inch) pieces
2 tablespoons peanut oil
½ teaspoon sesame oil
6 thin spring onions (scallions), cut
  into 3 cm (1¼ inch) lengths
1 carrot, thinly sliced on the diagonal
1 small green capsicum (pepper),
  thinly sliced
220 g (5 cups) Chinese cabbage
  (wom bok), shredded
nori sheets, finely julienned, to serve
  (optional)
pickled ginger, finely julienned,
  to serve (optional)

Sauce

60 ml (¼ cup) Japanese soy sauce
2 tablespoons Worcestershire sauce
1½ tablespoons rice vinegar
1 tablespoon sake
1 tablespoon mirin
1 tablespoon tomato sauce
1 tablespoon oyster sauce
2 teaspoons soft brown sugar

1 Place the Chinese mushrooms in a heatproof bowl, covering with boiling water. Soak for 20 minutes, or until soft. Drain, squeezing out any excess liquid and reserve 2 tablespoons of the soaking liquid. Discard the woody stems and thinly slice the caps.

2 Meanwhile, place the fillet slices in a bowl with half the garlic and half the ginger.

3 To make the sauce, combine all the ingredients in a bowl with the reserved mushroom liquid and the remaining garlic and ginger.

4 Place the noodles in a heatproof bowl, cover with boiling water and soak for 1 minute. Drain and separate.

5 Heat a wok over medium–high heat, add the bacon and cook for 2–3 minutes, or until softened and just starting to brown. Transfer to a large bowl. Combine the peanut and sesame oils. Increase the wok to high heat, add a little of the oil mixture and stir-fry the beef very quickly for 1 minute, or until it just changes colour all over. Add to the bacon.

6 Heat a little more oil mixture in the wok. Add the spring onion, carrot and capsicum and stir-fry for 1 minute. Add the cabbage and mushrooms and stir-fry for 30 seconds, or until the vegetables are just cooked but still crisp. Transfer to the bowl with the meat.

7 Heat the remaining oil in the wok. Stir-fry the noodles for 1 minute. Return the bacon, beef and vegetables to the wok, pour on the sauce and stir-fry for 2–3 minutes, or until combined and heated through (the sauce shouldn't be too runny, it should be almost completely absorbed but not dry). Divide among four deep bowls and top with nori and pickled ginger, if desired.

NUTRITION PER SERVE
Fat 30.5 g; Protein 44.5 g; Carbohydrate 75.5 g; Dietary Fibre 5 g; Cholesterol 113.5 mg; 3205 kJ (765 Cal)

Cut the fillet steak across the grain into thin slices.

Return the bacon, beef and prepared vegetables to the wok.

GREEN CURRY CHICKEN NOODLE STIR-FRY

Preparation time: 20 minutes
Cooking time: 15 minutes
Serves 4

400 g (14 oz) Hokkien egg noodles
1 tablespoon peanut oil
1 onion, cut into thin wedges
1½ tablespoons good-quality green
   curry paste
150 g (5½ oz) baby corn, cut in half
   on the diagonal
125 g (4½ oz) snake beans, cut into
   4 cm (1½ inch) lengths
250 ml (1 cup) coconut milk
125 ml (½ cup) chicken stock
500 g (1 lb 2 oz) chicken breast fillet,
   cut into 1 cm (½ inch) strips

2 teaspoons grated palm sugar
   or soft brown sugar
1 tablespoon fish sauce
2 teaspoons lime juice
3 tablespoons chopped coriander
   (cilantro) leaves
coriander (cilantro) leaves, extra,
   to garnish

1 Place the noodles in a heatproof bowl, cover with boiling water and soak for 1 minute, or until tender and separated. Drain well.
2 Heat a wok over high heat, add the oil and swirl to coat. Stir-fry the onion for 1–2 minutes, or until softened. Add the curry paste and cook for 1 minute, or until fragrant.
3 Add the baby corn, snake beans, coconut milk and stock to the wok

and simmer for 3–4 minutes. Add the chicken, and continue to cook for another 3–4 minutes, or until the chicken is cooked.
4 Stir the palm sugar, fish sauce and lime juice into the wok. Add the noodles and chopped coriander and toss until well combined and the noodles are warmed through. Serve immediately, garnished with the extra coriander leaves.

NUTRITION PER SERVE
Fat 28.5 g; Protein 41 g; Carbohydrate 65 g; Dietary Fibre 7 g; Cholesterol 95.5 mg; 2865 kJ (685 Cal)

BUDDHIST VEGETARIAN NOODLES

Preparation time: 25 minutes +
 20 minutes soaking
Cooking time: 15 minutes
Serves 4

15 g (1/2 oz) dried Chinese mushrooms
400 g (14 oz) fresh flat egg noodles
2–3 tablespoons peanut oil
1 small carrot, julienned
150 g (51/2 oz) baby corn, cut into
 quarters lengthways
230 g (8 oz) can julienned bamboo
 shoots, drained
150 g (51/2 oz) snow peas
 (mangetout), julienned
1/2 small red capsicum (pepper), julienned
1 small green capsicum (pepper),
 julienned
90 g (31/4 oz) bean sprouts, trimmed
40 g (11/2 oz) Chinese cabbage
 (wom bok), finely shredded
2 cm x 2 cm (3/4 inch x 3/4 inch) piece
 ginger, julienned
1 tablespoon mushroom soy sauce
1 tablespoon light soy sauce
1 tablespoon Chinese rice wine
2 tablespoons vegetarian oyster sauce
1 teaspoon sesame oil
ground white pepper, to taste
2 tablespoons coriander (cilantro) leaves

1 Place the Chinese mushrooms in a heatproof bowl, cover with boiling water and soak for 20 minutes. Drain. Discard the woody stems and thinly slice the caps.
2 Meanwhile, cook the noodles in a large saucepan of boiling water for 1 minute, stirring to separate. Drain. Rinse under cold, running water and drain again.
3 Heat a wok over high heat, add 1 tablespoon of the oil and swirl to coat. Stir-fry the carrot and corn for 1–2 minutes, then add the bamboo shoots and stir-fry for 1–2 minutes, or until just cooked but still crisp. Remove the vegetables to a side dish.
4 Reheat the wok (add 2 teaspoons peanut oil if necessary) and add the snow peas and red and green capsicum. Stir-fry for 1–2 minutes, or until just cooked but still crisp. Add to the carrot and corn mixture.

Reheat the wok (add another 2 teaspoons peanut oil if needed), then add the bean sprouts, cabbage and mushrooms and stir-fry for 30 seconds, or until wilted. Add the ginger and stir-fry for another 1–2 minutes. Remove and add to the other vegetables.
5 Heat the remaining oil in the wok, and quickly stir-fry the noodles for 1–2 minutes, or until heated through, taking care not to break them up. Stir

in the mushroom soy sauce, light soy sauce, rice wine and vegetarian oyster sauce. Return all the vegetables to the wok and stir gently for 1–2 minutes, or until well combined. Drizzle with the sesame oil, season with white pepper and garnish with the coriander leaves. Serve immediately.

NUTRITION PER SERVE
Fat 14.5 g; Protein 15 g; Carbohydrate 66 g; Dietary Fibre 7 g; Cholesterol 13 mg; 1925 kJ (460 Cal)

Cut the carrot into thin, even strips with a sharp knife.

Hold the cabbage firmly, then cut across to form even shreds.

HOKKIEN MEE

Preparation time: 20 minutes
Cooking time: 10 minutes
Serves 4

400 g (14 oz) Hokkien egg noodles
350 g (12 oz) medium prawns
    (shrimp)
2 tablespoons peanut oil
3 cloves garlic, finely chopped
200 g (7 oz) Chinese barbecued pork
    (char siu), thinly sliced
400 g (14 oz) baby bok choy (pak
    choi), trimmed and leaves
    separated
250 ml (1 cup) hot chicken stock
2 tablespoons dark soy sauce
1 tablespoon oyster sauce
½ teaspoon sugar
90 g (3¼ oz) bean sprouts

1 Place the noodles in a heatproof bowl, cover with boiling water and soak for 1 minute, or until tender and separated. Drain well and rinse.
2 To peel the prawns, remove the tails, and gently pull out the vein from the backs, starting at the head end, or slit the back and pull the vein out. Remove the tails.
3 Heat 1 tablespoon of the peanut oil in a wok over high heat. Add the prawns and garlic and cook for 1–2 minutes, or until just cooked through. Remove from the wok.
4 Heat the remaining oil in the wok over high heat, add the noodles, pork and bok choy and cook for 3–4 minutes, or until the bok choy has wilted but is still crisp. Add the chicken stock, soy and oyster sauces, and the sugar. Return the prawn and garlic mixture (with any juices) to the wok with the bean sprouts and stir quickly for 1–2 minutes, or until heated through.

NUTRITION PER SERVE
Fat 12.5 g; Protein 37 g; Carbohydrate 55.5 g; Dietary Fibre 4.5 g; Cholesterol 142 mg; 2040 kJ (490 Cal)

Pour the stock, sauces and sugar over the noodle and vegetable mixture.

SHANGHAI PORK NOODLES

Preparation time: 25 minutes +
  30 minutes marinating
Cooking time: 20 minutes
Serves 4

1/2 teaspoon sesame oil
60 ml (1/4 cup) light soy sauce
2 tablespoons oyster sauce
250 g (9 oz) pork loin, cut into thin
  strips across the grain
2 tablespoons dried shrimp
8 dried Chinese mushrooms
1 teaspoon sugar
250 ml (1 cup) chicken stock
300 g (10 1/2 oz) Shanghai noodles
2 tablespoons peanut oil
1 clove garlic, finely sliced
2 teaspoons grated ginger
1 celery stick, julienned
1 leek (white part only), julienned
150 g (5 1/2 oz) Chinese cabbage
  (wom bok), shredded
50 g (1 3/4 oz) canned bamboo shoots,
  drained and julienned
8 spring onions (scallions), thinly
  sliced

1 Combine the sesame oil,
1 tablespoon of the soy sauce and
1 tablespoon of the oyster sauce. Put
the pork in a non-metallic bowl, pour
the marinade on top and toss to coat
well. Cover and marinate for at least
30 minutes in the refrigerator.
2 Meanwhile, place the dried shrimp
in a bowl, cover with boiling water
and soak for 30 minutes. Drain and
finely chop.
3 Place the Chinese mushrooms in
a heatproof bowl, cover with boiling
water and soak for 20 minutes.
Drain, discard the stems and thinly
slice the caps.
4 Combine the sugar, chicken stock,
remaining soy and oyster sauces
and 1 teaspoon salt in a jug.
5 Cook the noodles in a large
saucepan of boiling water for
4–5 minutes, or until tender. Drain
and rinse under cold water. Toss
with 1 teaspoon peanut oil.
6 Heat a wok over high heat, add
1 tablespoon of the peanut oil and
swirl to coat. Add the pork and

stir-fry for 1–2 minutes, or until the
pork is no longer pink. Transfer to a
side plate. Heat the remaining peanut
oil, add the garlic, ginger, celery, leek
and cabbage and stir-fry for 1 minute,
or until softened. Add the bamboo
shoots, spring onion, mushrooms
and shrimp and stir-fry for 1 minute.
Add the noodles and the sauce
mixture, and toss together for

3–5 minutes, or until the noodles
absorb the sauce. Return the pork to
the wok, with any juices and toss
through for 1–2 minutes, or until
well combined and heated through.
Serve immediately.

NUTRITION PER SERVE
Fat 11.5 g; Protein 25.5 g; Carbohydrate
47 g; Dietary Fibre 4 g; Cholesterol 69 mg;
1675 kJ (400 Cal)

*Cut the pork loin into thin strips across
the grain.*

*Add the noodles to the wok, separating
with your hands.*

CHIANG MAI NOODLES

Preparation time: 30 minutes
Cooking time: 15 minutes
Serves 4

250 g (9 oz) fresh thin egg noodles
2 tablespoons oil
6 red Asian shallots, finely chopped
3 cloves garlic, crushed
1–2 small red chillies, seeded and
   finely chopped
2–3 tablespoons red curry paste
375 g (13 oz) chicken breast fillet, cut
   into thin strips
2 tablespoons fish sauce
1 tablespoon grated palm sugar
750 ml (3 cups) coconut milk
1 tablespoon lime juice
250 ml (1 cup) chicken stock

4 spring onions (scallions), sliced,
   to garnish
10 g (⅓ cup) coriander (cilantro)
   leaves
crisp fried shallots, to garnish
purchased fried noodles, to garnish
small red chilli, finely diced,
   to garnish

1 Cook the noodles in a saucepan of boiling water for 1 minute, or until tender. Drain, cover and set aside.
2 Heat a wok over high heat, add the oil and swirl to coat. Add the shallots, garlic and chilli, and stir-fry for 1–2 minutes, or until lightly golden. Stir in the curry paste and cook for 2 minutes, or until fragrant. Add the chicken and stir-fry for 3 minutes, or until almost cooked.

3 Stir in the fish sauce, palm sugar, coconut milk, lime juice and stock. Reduce the heat to low and simmer for 5 minutes—do not boil.
4 To serve, divide the noodles among four deep serving bowls and spoon the chicken mixture on top. Garnish with the spring onion, coriander leaves, crisp fried shallots, fried noodles and chilli.

NUTRITION PER SERVE
Fat 58.5 g; Protein 32 g; Carbohydrate 45.5 g; Dietary Fibre 6.5 g; Cholesterol 70 mg; 3475 kJ (830 Cal)

COOK'S FILE
Note: If you prefer a hotter flavoured dish, increase the amount of chilli and curry paste to your liking.

DAN DAN NOODLES

Preparation time: 15 minutes +
20 minutes marinating
Cooking time: 25 minutes
Serves 4

1 tablespoon Chinese rice wine
1/2 teaspoon sesame oil
1 teaspoon chilli oil
60 ml (1/4 cup) light soy sauce
500 g (1 lb 2 oz) minced (ground)
    chicken
1 tablespoon peanut oil
2 cloves garlic, finely chopped
1 teaspoon finely chopped ginger
2 teaspoons chilli bean paste
1 tablespoon Chinese sesame paste
185 ml (3/4 cup) chicken stock
1 tablespoon oyster sauce
375 g (13 oz) fresh flat egg noodles
3 spring onions (scallions), thinly
    sliced on the diagonal

1 Combine the rice wine, sesame oil, chilli oil and 2 tablespoons soy sauce in a bowl. Add the minced chicken and mix well. Cover with plastic wrap and marinate for 20 minutes.
2 Heat a wok over high heat, add the peanut oil and swirl to coat. Add the garlic, ginger and chilli bean paste and stir-fry for 1 minute, or until fragrant. Add the chicken mixture and cook for 2–3 minutes, or until browned, stirring to break up any lumps. Stir in the sesame paste, chicken stock, oyster sauce and remaining soy sauce, then reduce the heat to medium–low and simmer for 20 minutes.
3 Meanwhile, cook the noodles in a saucepan of boiling water for 1 minute, or until tender. Drain, rinse with cold water, then drain again. Divide among individual serving dishes (or place on a large,

warm serving platter).
4 Stir the spring onion through the chicken mixture, then spoon over the noodles. Serve immediately.

NUTRITION PER SERVE
Fat 20.5 g; Protein 36 g; Carbohydrate 52 g; Dietary Fibre 3.5 g; Cholesterol 124.5 mg; 2275 kJ (545 Cal)

Combine the minced chicken and the soy sauce mixture with a fork.

SEARED SCALLOPS WITH CHILLI BEAN PASTE

Preparation time: 20 minutes
Cooking time: 15 minutes
Serves 4

500 g (1 lb 2 oz) Hokkien egg noodles
60 ml (¼ cup) peanut oil
20 scallops, roe and beards removed
1 large onion, cut into thin wedges
3 cloves garlic, crushed
1 tablespoon grated ginger
1 tablespoon chilli bean paste
150 g (5½ oz) choy sum, cut into
    5 cm (2 inch) lengths
60 ml (¼ cup) chicken stock
2 tablespoons light soy sauce
2 tablespoons kecap manis
15 g (½ cup) coriander (cilantro)
    leaves
90 g (1 cup) bean sprouts
1 long red chilli, seeded and finely
    sliced
1 teaspoon sesame oil
1 tablespoon Chinese rice wine

1 Put the noodles in a heatproof bowl, cover with boiling water and soak for 1 minute until tender and separated. Drain, rinse under cold water, then drain again.

2 Heat a wok over high heat, add 2 tablespoons of the peanut oil and swirl to coat the side of the wok. Add the scallops in batches and sear for 20 seconds each side, or until sealed. Remove, then wipe the wok clean. Add the remaining oil and swirl to coat. Stir-fry the onion for 2 minutes, or until softened. Add the garlic and ginger and cook for 30 seconds. Stir in the chilli bean paste and cook for 1 minute, or until fragrant.

3 Add the choy sum to the wok with the noodles, stock, soy sauce and kecap manis. Stir-fry for 4 minutes, or until the choy sum has wilted and the noodles have absorbed most of the liquid. Return the scallops to the wok, add the coriander, bean sprouts, chilli, sesame oil and rice wine, tossing gently until combined.

NUTRITION PER SERVE
Fat 16 g; Protein 23.5 g; Carbohydrate 71 g; Dietary Fibre 5 g; Cholesterol 37.5 mg; 2225 kJ (530 Cal)

Remove the seeds and membrane from the chilli.

Return the scallops to the wok, then stir-fry until well combined and heated through.

ASIAN ROASTED DUCK WITH RICE NOODLES

Preparation time: 25 minutes
Cooking time: 15 minutes
Serves 4

1.5 kg (3 lb 5 oz) Chinese roast duck
500 g (1 lb 2 oz) fresh flat rice
   noodles (1 cm or 1/2 inch wide)
3 1/2 tablespoons peanut oil
3 small (180 g or 6 oz) slender
   eggplants (aubergines), cut into
   1 cm (1/2 inch) thick slices
2 cm x 2 cm (3/4 inch x 3/4 inch) piece
   ginger, julienned
2 small red chillies, finely chopped
4 spring onions (scallions), thinly
   sliced on the diagonal
3 tablespoons torn basil
60 ml (1/4 cup) Chinese barbecue
   sauce

1 Remove the crispy skin and meat from the duck, discarding the carcass and fat. Finely slice the meat and skin. Place in a bowl—there should be at least 350 g (12 oz) of meat.

2 Place the noodles in a heatproof bowl, cover with boiling water and soak briefly. Gently separate the noodles with your hands. Rinse under cold water and drain well.

3 Heat a wok over high heat, add 2 1/2 tablespoons of the peanut oil and swirl to coat. When hot, add the eggplant and stir-fry for 3–4 minutes, or until softened. Transfer to a bowl.

4 Heat the remaining oil in the wok over high heat. Cook the ginger, chilli and spring onion for 30 seconds, stirring constantly. Return the eggplant to the wok. Add the duck, basil and barbecue sauce, and gently toss together for 1–2 minutes, or until heated through. Add the noodles and stir-fry for 1–2 minutes, or until well combined and heated through, taking care not to break up the noodles. Serve immediately.

NUTRITION PER SERVE
Fat 39.5 g; Protein 24.5 g; Carbohydrate 60.5 g; Dietary Fibre 3 g; Cholesterol 115.5 mg; 2900 kJ (695 Cal)

Rinse the soaked noodles under cold running water, then drain well.

CHICKEN CHOW MEIN

Preparation time: 15 minutes +
　1 hour standing
Cooking time: 40 minutes
Serves 4

250 g (9 oz) fresh thin egg noodles
2 teaspoons sesame oil
125 ml (1/2 cup) peanut oil
400 g (14 oz) chicken breast fillet,
　cut into thin strips
1 tablespoon Chinese rice wine
1 1/2 tablespoons light soy sauce
3 teaspoons cornflour (cornstarch)
1 clove garlic, crushed
1 tablespoon finely chopped ginger
100 g (3 1/2 oz) sugar snap peas, trimmed
250 g (9 oz) finely shredded Chinese
　cabbage (wom bok)
4 spring onions (scallions), cut into
　2 cm (3/4 inch) lengths
100 ml (3 1/2 fl oz) chicken stock
1 1/2 tablespoons oyster sauce
100 g (3 1/2 oz) bean sprouts
1 small red chilli, seeded and
　julienned, to garnish (optional)

1 Cook the noodles in a saucepan of boiling water for 1 minute, or until tender. Drain well. Add the sesame oil and 1 tablespoon of the peanut oil to the noodles and toss well. Place on a baking tray and spread out to a thin layer. Leave in a dry place for at least 1 hour.
2 Meanwhile, place the chicken in a large bowl. Combine the rice wine, 1 tablespoon of the soy sauce and 1 teaspoon of the cornflour. Pour over the chicken and toss to coat well. Cover and marinate for 10 minutes.
3 Heat 1 tablespoon of the peanut oil in a small non-stick frying pan over high heat. Add one-quarter of the noodles, shaping into a pancake, then reduce the heat to medium and cook for 4 minutes each side, or until crisp and golden. Drain on crumpled paper towels and keep warm. Repeat with 3 tablespoons of the oil and the remaining noodles to make four noodle cakes in total.
4 Heat a wok over high heat, add the remaining peanut oil and swirl to coat. Stir-fry the garlic and ginger for 30 seconds. Add the chicken and

stir-fry for 3–4 minutes, or until golden and tender. Add the sugar snap peas, shredded cabbage and spring onion and stir-fry well for 2 minutes, or until the cabbage has wilted. Stir in the chicken stock, oyster sauce and bean sprouts and bring to the boil.
5 Combine the remaining cornflour with 1–2 teaspoons cold water. Stir it into the wok with the remaining soy sauce and cook for 1–2 minutes, or until the sauce thickens.
6 To assemble, place a noodle cake on each serving plate, then spoon the chicken and vegetable mixture on top. Serve immediately, garnished with chilli, if desired.

NUTRITION PER SERVE
Fat 39.5 g; Protein 31 g; Carbohydrate 39.5 g; Dietary Fibre 4 g; Cholesterol 74 mg; 2685 kJ (640 Cal)

Cook the noodle pancake on both sides until crisp and golden.

CHILLI SNAKE BEANS AND NOODLES

Preparation time: 15 minutes
Cooking time: 10 minutes
Serves 4

325 g (11 1/2 oz) fresh flat egg noodles
(5 mm or 1/4 inch wide)
5 cloves garlic, peeled
3 red Asian shallots, chopped
1 small red chilli, seeded and chopped
3 coriander (cilantro) roots, chopped
2 1/2 tablespoons peanut oil
500 g (1 lb 2 oz) snake beans, cut
into 4 cm (1 1/2 inch) lengths
2 1/2 tablespoons fish sauce
1 1/2 tablespoons grated palm sugar
1 tablespoon kecap manis
1 tablespoon lime juice
1 tablespoon crisp fried onion flakes
1 small red chilli, extra, thinly sliced
lime wedges, to serve

1 Cook the noodles in a saucepan of boiling water for 1 minute, or until tender. Drain well.

2 Place the garlic, red Asian shallots, chilli and coriander roots in a mortar and pestle or small food processor and grind to a smooth paste—add a little water if necessary.

3 Heat a wok over high heat, add the oil and swirl to coat. Stir in the paste and cook for 1 minute, or until fragrant. Add the beans, stir-fry for 2 minutes, then reduce the heat to low, cover and steam for 2 minutes. Increase the heat to high, add the fish sauce, palm sugar and kecap manis and stir-fry for 1 minute. Toss the noodles through the bean mixture for 1–2 minutes, or until heated through. Drizzle with the lime juice. Divide among four serving bowls, garnish with the crisp fried onion flakes and chilli and serve with lime wedges.

NUTRITION PER SERVE
Fat 12.5 g; Protein 12 g; Carbohydrate 52 g; Dietary Fibre 6 g; Cholesterol 10.5 mg; 1555 kJ (370 Cal)

Stir-fry the snake beans and the paste until well combined.

KIM CHI PICKLED VEGETABLES WITH OMELETTE ON POTATO STARCH NOODLES

Preparation time: 20 minutes
Cooking time: 10 minutes
Serves 6 (as a side dish)

200 g (7 oz) potato starch noodles (Korean vermicelli)
1½ tablespoons vegetable oil
2 eggs, separated
1 teaspoon sugar
1 tablespoon light soy sauce
1 teaspoon sesame oil
2 spring onions (scallions), thinly sliced on the diagonal
160 g (1 cup) prepared Kim chi pickled vegetables (see Note)

1 Cook the noodles in a saucepan of boiling water for 3 minutes, or until softened. Drain and rinse under cold, running water.

2 Heat a wok over high heat, add 2 teaspoons of the oil and swirl to coat. Lightly beat the egg yolks, season and cook, undisturbed, for 30 seconds, then turn to cook the other side for 30 seconds. Transfer to a plate. Lightly beat the egg white, season and cook the same way as the yolks. Slice the egg yolk and egg white into thin strips, about 3 cm (1¼ inch) long.

3 Heat the remaining oil in the wok, add the noodles, sugar, soy sauce, sesame oil and spring onion and stir-fry for 1 minute. Top with the egg strips and pickled vegetables and serve immediately.

NUTRITION PER SERVE
Fat 7.5 g; Protein 6.5 g; Carbohydrate 24 g; Dietary Fibre 2 g; Cholesterol 67.5 mg; 790 kJ (190 Cal)

COOK'S FILE
Note: Kim chi is a hot, fermented vegetable pickle, most commonly made with cabbage. It can be purchased in packets or tubs in the refrigerated section of Asian grocery stores.

Slice the egg yolk and egg white omelettes into thin strips.

FRIED NOODLES INDONESIAN STYLE (BAHMI GORENG)

Preparation time: 25 minutes
Cooking time: 20 minutes
Serves 4

400 g (14 oz) fresh flat egg noodles (5 mm or 1/4 inch wide)
2 tablespoons peanut oil
4 red Asian shallots, thinly sliced
2 cloves garlic, chopped
1 small red chilli, finely diced
200 g (7 oz) pork fillet, thinly sliced across the grain
200 g (7 oz) chicken breast fillet, thinly sliced
200 g (7 oz) small prawns (shrimp), peeled, deveined and tails intact
2 Chinese cabbage (wom bok) leaves, shredded
2 carrots, cut in half lengthways and thinly sliced
100 g (3 1/2 oz) snake beans, cut into 3 cm (1 1/4 inch) lengths
60 ml (1/4 cup) kecap manis
1 tablespoon light soy sauce
2 tomatoes, peeled, seeded and chopped
4 spring onions (scallions), sliced on the diagonal
1 tablespoon crisp fried onion flakes
flat-leaf (Italian) parsley, to garnish

1 Cook the noodles in a large saucepan of boiling water for 1 minute, or until tender. Drain and rinse under cold water.
2 Heat a wok over high heat, add the peanut oil and swirl to coat. Stir-fry the red Asian shallots for 30 seconds. Add the garlic, chilli and pork and stir-fry for 2 minutes, then add the chicken and cook a further 2 minutes, or until the meat is golden and tender. Add the prawns and stir-fry for another 2 minutes, or until pink and just cooked. Stir in the cabbage, carrot and beans and cook for 3 minutes, then add the noodles and gently stir-fry for 4 minutes, or until heated through—taking care not to break up the noodles. Stir in the kecap manis, soy sauce, chopped tomato and spring onion and stir-fry for 1–2 minutes. Season to taste with salt and freshly ground black pepper. Garnish with crisp fried onion flakes and parsley, and serve immediately.

NUTRITION PER SERVE
Fat 14 g; Protein 44.5 g; Carbohydrate 58 g; Dietary Fibre 5.5 g; Cholesterol 168 mg; 2280 kJ (545 Cal)

COOK'S FILE
Note: This dish is traditionally eaten with chopped roasted peanuts and sambal oelek on the side. It is also delicious with satay sauce.
Variation: Use 300 g (10 1/2 oz) chicken and omit the prawns, if desired.

SPICY CHILLI PRAWNS WITH HOKKIEN NOODLES

Preparation time: 15 minutes
Cooking time: 10 minutes
Serves 4

400 g (14 oz) Hokkien egg noodles
1 tablespoon peanut oil
1 tablespoon red curry paste
2 cloves garlic, crushed
1 stem lemon grass (white part only),
    finely chopped
2 tablespoons finely sliced coriander
    (cilantro) root
125 ml (1/2 cup) lime juice
60 g (1/3 cup) grated palm sugar
2 tablespoons tomato sauce
2 1/2 tablespoons fish sauce
185 ml (3/4 cup) chicken stock
16 medium prawns (shrimp), peeled
    and deveined
350 g (12 oz) choy sum, cut into
    2 cm (3/4 inch) lengths

100 g (3 1/2 oz) snake beans, cut into
    1.5 cm (5/8 inch) lengths
4 spring onions (scallions), finely
    chopped
115 g (3/4 cup) roasted cashew nuts,
    roughly chopped
15 g (1/2 cup) coriander (cilantro)
    leaves
Thai basil, to garnish
lime wedges, to serve (optional)

1 Place the noodles in a large heatproof bowl, cover with boiling water and soak for 1 minute, or until tender and separated. Drain well, rinse under cold water and drain again.
2 Heat a wok over high heat, add the oil and swirl to coat. Add the curry paste and fry for 5 seconds, then add the garlic, lemon grass and coriander root and stir-fry for 30 seconds, or until well combined and fragrant.
3 Whisk the lime juice, palm sugar,

tomato sauce, fish sauce and stock together, then add to the wok. Cook over high heat for 2 minutes, or until slightly reduced. Add the prawns and cook for 2–3 minutes, or until almost cooked. Add the noodles and stir-fry for 2 minutes. Add the choy sum and beans and continue to stir-fry for 2 minutes, or until the leaves have wilted and the beans are tender but not soft. Stir in the spring onion, cashews and coriander leaves until combined. Garnish with the basil and serve immediately with lime wedges, if desired.

NUTRITION PER SERVE
Fat 21.5 g; Protein 29 g; Carbohydrate 80 g; Dietary Fibre 6.5 g; Cholesterol 95 mg; 2655 kJ (635 Cal)

PORK AND PRAWN VERMICELLI

Preparation time: 25 minutes +
  10 minutes soaking
Cooking time: 10 minutes
Serves 4

100 g (3½ oz) dried rice vermicelli
2 tablespoons peanut oil
200 g (7 oz) lean minced (ground)
  pork
100 g (3½ oz) red Asian shallots,
  finely chopped
2 cloves garlic, finely chopped
2 small red chillies, finely chopped
100 g (3½ oz) Chinese celery or
  celery, finely chopped
12 medium prawns (shrimp), peeled
  and deveined
1 makrut (kaffir) lime leaf, shredded
1½ tablespoons fish sauce
1 tablespoon sugar
2½ tablespoons lime juice

2 tablespoons mint
3 tablespoons Thai basil
4 tablespoons coriander (cilantro)
  leaves

1 Place the vermicelli in a large heatproof bowl, cover with boiling water and soak for 6–7 minutes, or until tender. Drain well and set aside.
2 Heat a wok until very hot, add 1 tablespoon of the oil and swirl to coat. Add the minced pork and stir-fry for 1–2 minutes, or until slightly brown, stirring to break up any lumps. Drain and transfer to a plate lined with paper towel.
3 Heat the remaining oil in the wok over high heat and stir-fry the shallots, garlic, chilli and celery for 1 minute. Add the prawns, lime leaf, fish sauce, sugar and lime juice and continue to stir-fry for 1 minute, or until the prawns start to turn pink.

4 Add the vermicelli and pork to the wok and stir-fry for 1–2 minutes, or until well combined and heated through. Divide among the serving dishes, then toss in the mint, basil and coriander. Serve immediately.

NUTRITION PER SERVE
Fat 12.5 g; Protein 21.5 g; Carbohydrate 22.5 g; Dietary Fibre 2 g; Cholesterol 91.5 mg; 1215 kJ (290 Cal)

COOK'S FILE
Note: It is important to toss the herbs through the stir-fry after the mixture has been transferred to the serving bowls—if the herbs are tossed through in the wok, the heat of the wok will cause them to wilt very quickly and they will lose their aesthetic quality.

HOTPOTS

LAMB HOTPOT WITH RICE NOODLES

Preparation time: 20 minutes +
  2 hours marinating
Cooking time: 2 hours
Serves 4

2 cloves garlic, crushed
2 teaspoons grated ginger
1 teaspoon five-spice powder
1/4 teaspoon ground white pepper
2 tablespoons Chinese rice wine
1 teaspoon sugar
1 kg (2 lb 4 oz) boneless lamb shoulder,
  cut into 3 cm (1 1/4 inch) pieces
30 g (1 oz) dried Chinese mushrooms
1 tablespoon peanut oil
1 large onion, cut into wedges
2 cm (3/4 inch) piece ginger, julienned
1 teaspoon Sichuan peppercorns,
  crushed or ground
2 tablespoons sweet bean paste
1 teaspoon black peppercorns,
  toasted and ground
500 ml (2 cups) chicken stock
60 ml (1/4 cup) oyster sauce
2 star anise
60 ml (1/4 cup) Chinese rice wine, extra
80 g (3 oz) can sliced bamboo
  shoots, drained
100 g (3 1/2 oz) can water chestnuts,
  drained and sliced
400 g (14 oz) fresh rice noodles, cut
  into 2 cm (3/4 inch) wide strips

1 spring onion (scallion), sliced on
  the diagonal

1 Combine the garlic, grated ginger, five-spice powder, white pepper, rice wine, sugar and 1 teaspoon salt in a large bowl. Add the lamb and toss to coat. Cover and marinate for 2 hours.
2 Meanwhile, soak the mushrooms in boiling water for 20 minutes. Drain. Discard the stems and slice the caps.
3 Heat a wok over high heat, then add the oil. Stir-fry the onion, julienned ginger and Sichuan pepper for 2 minutes. Cook the lamb in batches, stir-frying for 3 minutes, or until starting to brown. Stir in the bean paste and ground peppercorn. Cook for 3 minutes, until the lamb is brown. Add the stock and transfer to a 2 litre (8 cup) flameproof clay pot or casserole dish. Stir in the oyster sauce, star anise and extra rice wine. Simmer, covered, over low heat for 1 1/2 hours, or until the lamb is tender. Stir in the bamboo shoots and water chestnuts. Cook for 20 minutes. Add the mushrooms.
4 Cover the noodles with boiling water and separate. Drain and rinse. Add to the hotpot and stir until heated. Sprinkle with spring onion.

NUTRITION PER SERVE
Fat 20.5 g; Protein 58 g; Carbohydrate 56.5 g; Dietary Fibre 4 g; Cholesterol 167.5 mg; 2805 kJ (670 Cal)

Stir the bean paste into the lamb and onion mixture.

Stir the bamboo shoots and water chestnuts into the hotpot.

ROAST PORK, CHINESE CABBAGE AND NOODLE HOTPOT

Preparation time: 10 minutes +
  5 minutes soaking
Cooking time: 20 minutes
Serves 4

70 g (2½ oz) mung bean vermicelli
250 g (9 oz) Chinese cabbage
  (wom bok)
1 litre (4 cups) chicken stock
2.5 cm x 2.5 cm (1 inch x 1 inch)
  piece ginger, thinly sliced
350 g (12 oz) Chinese roast pork,
  skin removed and reserved
  2 spring onions (scallions), thinly
  sliced on the diagonal
2 tablespoons light soy sauce
1 tablespoon Chinese rice wine
½ teaspoon sesame oil
100 g (3½ oz) Sichuan pickles,
  roughly chopped (optional)

1 Soak the vermicelli in boiling water for 3–4 minutes. Drain and rinse then drain again.

2 Separate the cabbage leaves and cut the leafy ends from the stems. Cut both the cabbage stems and the leaves into 2–3 cm (1–1¼ inch) squares.

3 Pour the chicken stock and into a 2 litre (8 cup) flameproof casserole dish and add the ginger slices. Bring to the boil over high heat. Add the cabbage stems and cook for 2 minutes, then add the cabbage leaves and cook for a further 1 minute. Reduce the heat to medium, add the noodles and cook, covered, for 4–5 minutes, stirring occasionally.

4 Meanwhile, cut the pork into 2 cm (¾ inch) cubes and add to the pan with the spring onion, soy sauce, rice wine and sesame oil. Stir to combine, then cook, covered, for

a further 3–4 minutes. Serve with the pickles served on the side.

NUTRITION PER SERVE
Fat 4.5 g; Protein 31.5 g; Carbohydrate 13 g; Dietary Fibre 2.5 g; Cholesterol 112 mg; 950 kJ (225 Cal)

Cut the Chinese cabbage leaves and stems into cubes.

SHABU SHABU

Preparation time: 20 minutes +
   40 minutes freezing
Cooking time: 10 minutes
Serves 4

300 g (10½ oz) beef fillet, trimmed
1.5 litres (6 cups) chicken stock
2 cm x 6 cm (¾ inch x 2½ inch)
   piece ginger, thinly sliced
80 ml (⅓ cup) light soy sauce
2 tablespoons mirin
1 teaspoon sesame oil
200 g (7 oz) fresh udon noodles
150 g (5½ oz) English spinach, stems
   removed and thinly sliced
400 g (14 oz) Chinese cabbage (wom
   bok), leaves only, finely shredded
100 g (3½ oz) fresh shiitake
   mushrooms, stems removed and
   caps thinly sliced
200 g (7 oz) firm tofu, cut into 2 cm
   (¾ inch) cubes
80 ml (⅓ cup) ready-made ponzu sauce
   or 60 ml (¼ cup) soy sauce mixed
   with 1 tablespoon lemon juice

1 Wrap the beef fillet in plastic wrap and freeze for 40 minutes, or until it begins to harden. Remove and slice as thinly as possible across the grain.
2 Place the stock, ginger, soy sauce, mirin and sesame oil in a 2.5 litre (10 cup) flameproof casserole dish or hotpot over medium heat and simmer for 3 minutes. Add the noodles, stir to separate gently with chopsticks and cook for 1–2 minutes. Add spinach, cabbage, mushrooms and tofu and simmer for 1 minute, or until the leaves have wilted.
3 Divide the noodles among four serving bowls using tongs, and top with the beef slices, vegetables and tofu. Ladle the hot stock on top and serve the ponzu sauce on the side.

NUTRITION PER SERVE
Fat 10.5 g; Protein 37.5 g; Carbohydrate 40.5 g; Dietary Fibre 7.5 g; Cholesterol 50 mg; 1800 kJ (430 Cal)

COOK'S FILE
Note: Traditionally, raw beef slices are arranged on a plate with the tofu, mushrooms, vegetables and noodles. The stock and seasoning are heated on a portable gas flame at the table. Guests dip the meat and vegetables in the hot stock and eat as they go, dipping into the dipping sauce. The noodles are added at the end and served with the broth.

Cut the partially frozen beef fillet as thinly as possible.

LION'S HEAD MEATBALLS

Preparation time: 20 minutes +
  overnight refrigeration +
  20 minutes soaking
Cooking time: 4 hours 45 minutes
Serves 4

Chicken stock
1.5 kg (3 lb 5 oz) chicken bones
  (necks, backs, wings), washed
2 slices ginger, 1 cm (1/2 inch) thick
4 spring onions (scallions), white
  part only

6 dried Chinese mushrooms
100 g (3 1/2 oz) mung bean vermicelli
600 g (1 lb 5 oz) minced (ground)
  pork
1 egg white
4 cloves garlic, finely chopped
1 tablespoon finely grated ginger
1 tablespoon cornflour (cornstarch)
1 1/2 tablespoons Chinese rice wine
6 spring onions (scallions), thinly
  sliced
2 tablespoons peanut oil
60 ml (1/4 cup) light soy sauce
1 teaspoon sugar
400 g (14 oz) bok choy (pak choi),
  cut in half lengthways and
  leaves separated

1 To make the stock, put the bones and 3.5 litres (14 cups) water in a large saucepan and bring to a simmer—do not let it boil. Remove the scum from the surface and continue doing so over the next 30 minutes. Add the ginger and spring onion and cook, partially covered, keeping at a low simmer for 3 hours. Strain through a fine sieve. Cool. Cover and refrigerate overnight. Remove the layer of fat from the surface once it has solidified.
2 Soak the Chinese mushrooms in 250 ml (1 cup) boiling water for 20 minutes. Drain. Discard the stems and thinly slice the caps. Meanwhile, place the vermicelli in a heatproof bowl, cover with boiling water and soak for 3–4 minutes, or until soft. Drain and rinse. Preheat the oven to hot 220°C (425°F/Gas 7).
3 Place the minced pork, egg white, garlic, ginger, cornflour, rice wine,

two-thirds of the spring onion and salt to taste in a food processor. Using the pulse button, process until smooth and well combined. Divide the mixture into eight portions and shape into large balls with wet hands.
4 Place 500 ml (2 cups) of the stock (freeze any remaining stock) in a large saucepan and bring to the boil over high heat, then remove from the heat and keep warm.
5 Heat the oil in a wok over high heat. Fry the meatballs in batches for 2 minutes each side, or until golden,

but not cooked through. Drain.
6 Place the meatballs, mushrooms, soy sauce and sugar in a 2.5 litre (10 cup) flameproof clay pot or casserole dish and cover with the hot stock. Bake, covered, for 45 minutes. Add the bok choy and noodles and bake, covered, for another 10 minutes. Sprinkle with the remaining spring onion and serve.

NUTRITION PER SERVE
Fat 19.5 g; Protein 35 g; Carbohydrate 21.5 g; Dietary Fibre 4 g; Cholesterol 96.5 mg; 1720 kJ (410 Cal)

Form the minced pork mixture into eight large balls using wet hands.

Add the bok choy and noodles to the clay pot containing the meatballs.

FISH HOTPOT WITH GINGER AND TOMATOES

Preparation time: 20 minutes +
　20 minutes soaking
Cooking time: 1 hour
Serves 4

1 tablespoon peanut oil
1 onion, cut into thin wedges
1 small red chilli, sliced
3 cloves garlic, finely chopped
2 cm x 2 cm (3/4 inch x 3/4 inch) piece
　ginger, julienned
1/2 teaspoon ground turmeric
425 g (15 oz) can diced tomatoes
1 litre (4 cups) chicken stock
1 tablespoon tamarind purée
80 g (3 oz) dried flat rice stick noodles
600 g (1lb 5 oz) snapper (or firm white
　fish) fillets, skin removed, cut into
　3 cm (1¼ inch) cubes

coriander (cilantro) leaves,
　to garnish

1 Preheat the oven to hot 220°C (425°F/Gas 7). Heat the oil in a frying pan over medium–high heat, and cook the onion for 1–2 minutes, or until softened. Add the chilli, garlic and ginger and cook for a further 30 seconds. Add the ground turmeric, tomato, chicken stock and tamarind purée and bring to the boil over high heat. Transfer to a 2.5 litre (10 cup) heatproof hotpot or flameproof casserole dish and cook, covered, in the oven for 40 minutes.
2 Place the noodles in a large heatproof bowl, cover with warm water and soak for 15–20 minutes, or until *al dente*. Drain, rinse and drain again.
3 Remove the hotpot from the oven

and stir in the noodles. Add the fish cubes, then cover and return to the oven for a further 10 minutes, or until the fish is cooked through. Serve sprinkled with coriander.

NUTRITION PER SERVE
Fat 8 g; Protein 36 g; Carbohydrate 23.5 g; Dietary Fibre 3 g; Cholesterol 91.5 mg; 1310 kJ (315 Cal)

Gently add the fish cubes to the hotpot mixture.

103

NABEYAKI UDON

Preparation time: 20 minutes +
   5 minutes soaking
Cooking time: 20 minutes
Serves 4

250 g (9 oz) fresh udon noodles
2 teaspoons dashi granules
80 ml (1/3 cup) Japanese soy sauce
1 tablespoon sugar
2 tablespoons mirin
4 large fresh shiitake mushrooms,
   stems removed and caps cut into
   1 cm (1/2 inch) slices
1 chicken breast fillet, cut into
   1 cm (1/2 inch) slices
8 medium prawns (shrimp), peeled,
   deveined and tails intact
1 Kamaboko pink fish cake, thinly
   sliced (see Note)
4 eggs, lightly beaten
2 spring onions (scallions), thinly sliced

1 Cook the noodles in a large saucepan of boiling water for 1–2 minutes, or until tender. Drain and rinse well.

2 Combine the dashi granules with 1 litre (4 cups) water in a large saucepan. Bring to the boil over high heat and stir to dissolve. Add the soy sauce, sugar, mirin and 2 teaspoons salt, then reduce heat and simmer.

3 Place the noodles, mushrooms, chicken, prawns and fish cake in a 1.5 litre (6 cup) flameproof casserole dish. Pour the hot broth on top and simmer, covered, over medium heat, for 3–5 minutes, or until the prawns and chicken are cooked through and tender.

4 Gently pour the egg into the centre of the mixture and continue to cook for 2 minutes, or until the egg has just set. Sprinkle with spring onion and serve immediately.

NUTRITION PER SERVE
Fat 12 g; Protein 36.5 g; Carbohydrate 25.5 g; Dietary Fibre 3 g; Cholesterol 306.5 mg; 1515 kJ (360 Cal)

COOK'S FILE
Notes: Kamaboko fish cakes are available from Japanese supermarkets. Individual flameproof casserole dishes or nabes can be used and are about 400 ml (14 fl oz) in size.

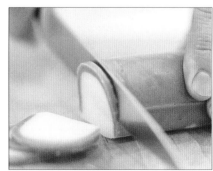

Hold the Kamaboko fish cake down firmly, then cut into thin slices.

CARAMEL PORK WITH SHANGHAI NOODLES

Preparation time: 15 minutes
Cooking time: 2 hours 30 minutes
Serves 4

500 g (1 lb 2 oz) Shanghai noodles
700 g (1 lb 9 oz) boneless pork belly
2 teaspoons peanut oil
150 g (5½ oz) caster (superfine) sugar
5 cloves garlic, crushed
5 slices ginger, 5 mm (⅛ inch) thick
2 stems lemon grass (white part only), bruised
1 teaspoon ground white pepper
500 ml (2 cups) chicken stock
3½ tablespoons fish sauce
100 g (3½ oz) canned bamboo shoots, drained well
4 spring onions (scallions), cut into 3 cm (1¼ inch) pieces
1 tablespoon lime juice
1 tablespoon chopped coriander (cilantro) leaves (optional)

1 Cook the noodles in a large pan of boiling water for 4–5 minutes, or until tender. Rinse, drain and cut into 10 cm (4 inch) lengths.
2 Preheat the oven to moderate 180°C (350°F/Gas 4). Cut the pork belly across the grain into 1 cm (½ inch) thick slices, then cut each slice into 2 cm (¾ inch) pieces. Heat the oil in a 4 litre (16 cup) clay pot or flameproof casserole dish over medium–high heat. Cook the pork in two batches for about 5 minutes, or until it starts to brown all over. Remove the pork and drain the fat.
3 Add the sugar and 2 tablespoons water to the casserole dish, stirring until the sugar has dissolved. Scrape up any sediment that has stuck to the bottom. Increase the heat to high and cook for 2–3 minutes without stirring until dark golden, being careful not to burn—you should just be able to smell the caramel.
4 Return the pork to the casserole dish, then add the garlic, ginger, lemon grass, white pepper, stock, 2 tablespoons of the fish sauce and 375 ml (1½ cups) water and stir to combine. Bake, covered, for 1 hour then remove the lid and cook for another hour, or until the pork is very tender. Carefully remove the ginger slices and the lemon grass.
5 Add the noodles to the casserole dish with the bamboo shoots, spring onion, lime juice and the remaining fish sauce and stir to combine. Return the dish to the oven for a further 10 minutes to heat through. Stir in the chopped coriander, if desired, and serve immediately with steamed Asian greens.

NUTRITION PER SERVE
Fat 7.5 g; Protein 48.5 g; Carbohydrate 73 g; Dietary Fibre 4 g; Cholesterol 166 mg; 2305 kJ (550 Cal)

Cut the pork belly across the grain into thick slices.

Return the browned pork pieces to the hotpot.

Remove the ginger slices and lemon grass from the hotpot.

105

TOFU PUFFS WITH SHIITAKE MUSHROOMS AND ROUND RICE NOODLES

Preparation time: 10 minutes +
  20 minutes soaking
Cooking time: 15 minutes
Serves 4

8 dried shiitake mushrooms
500 g (1 lb 2 oz) fresh round rice
  noodles
3 litres (12 cups) good-quality
  chicken stock
1 carrot, thinly sliced on the diagonal
100 g (3¹/2 oz) fried tofu puffs, cut in half
800 g (1 lb 12 oz) bok choy
  (pak choi), trimmed and quartered

1–1¹/2 tablespoons mushroom
  soy sauce
6 drops sesame oil
ground white pepper, to season
100 g (3¹/2 oz) enoki mushrooms,
  ends trimmed

1 Place the shiitake mushrooms in a heatproof bowl, cover with boiling water and soak for 20 minutes. Drain and remove the stems, squeezing out any excess water.
2 Meanwhile, place the noodles in a heatproof bowl, cover with boiling water and soak briefly. Gently separate the noodles with your hands and drain well.
3 Place the chicken stock in a large saucepan, cover and slowly heat

through over low heat.
4 Add the noodles to the simmering stock along with the carrot, tofu puffs, shiitake mushrooms and bok choy. Cook for 1–2 minutes, or until the carrot and noodles are tender and the bok choy has wilted slightly. Stir in the soy sauce and sesame oil and season to taste with white pepper.
5 Divide the noodles, vegetables, tofu puffs and enoki mushrooms among four serving bowls, ladle the broth on top and serve immediately.

NUTRITION PER SERVE
Fat 8.5 g; Protein 19.5 g; Carbohydrate
68.5 g; Dietary Fibre 9.5 g; Cholesterol
38.5 mg; 1825 kJ (435 Cal)

MONGOLIAN HOTPOT

Preparation time: 15 minutes +
    10 minutes soaking
Cooking time: 5 minutes
Serves 6

250 g (9 oz) dried rice vermicelli
600 g (1 lb 5 oz) lamb backstraps
    or loin fillets, thinly sliced across
    the grain
4 spring onions (scallions), sliced
1.5 litres (6 cups) light chicken
    stock
3 cm x 6 cm (1 1/4 inch x 2 1/2 inch)
    piece ginger, cut into 6 slices
2 tablespoons Chinese rice wine
300 g (10 1/2 oz) silken firm tofu, cut
    into 1.5 cm (5/8 inch) cubes
300 g (10 1/2 oz) Chinese broccoli (gai
    lan), cut into 4 cm (1 1/2 inch)
    lengths
75 g (2 cups) shredded Chinese
    cabbage (wom bok)

Sauce
80 ml (1/3 cup) light soy sauce
2 tablespoons Chinese sesame paste
1 tablespoon Chinese rice wine
1 teaspoon chilli and garlic paste

1 Place the vermicelli in a large heatproof bowl, cover with boiling water and soak for 6–7 minutes. Drain well and divide among six serving bowls. Top with the lamb slices and spring onion.
2 To make the sauce, combine the soy sauce, sesame paste, rice wine and the chilli and garlic paste in a small bowl.
3 Place the stock, ginger and rice wine in a 2.5 litre (10 cup) flameproof hotpot or large saucepan. Cover and bring to the boil over high heat. Add the tofu, Chinese broccoli and Chinese cabbage and simmer, uncovered, for 1 minute, or until the broccoli has wilted. Divide the tofu, broccoli and cabbage among the serving bowls, then ladle on the hot stock. Drizzle a little of the sauce on top and serve the rest on the side.

NUTRITION PER SERVE
Fat 16 g; Protein 35.5 g; Carbohydrate 32 g; Dietary Fibre 4 g; Cholesterol 68 mg; 1770 kJ (425 Cal)

COOK'S FILE
Notes: Make sure the stock is hot enough to cook the thin slices of lamb. This recipe traditionally uses a Chinese steamboat—this is an aluminium pot with a steam spout in the middle, placed on a propane burner in the middle of the dining table. You could also use a fondue pot instead.

SUKIYAKI

Preparation time: 10 minutes
Cooking time: 10 minutes
Serves 4

Sauce
1/2–1 teaspoon dashi granules
80 ml (1/3 cup) soy sauce
2 tablespoons sake
2 tablespoons mirin
1 tablespoon caster (superfine) sugar

300 g (10 1/2 oz) shirataki noodles
  (see Notes)
50 g (1 3/4 oz) lard
5 large spring onions (scallions), cut into
  1 cm (1/2 inch) slices on the diagonal
16 fresh shiitake mushrooms (180 g
  or 6 oz), cut into smaller pieces if
  too large
800 g (1 lb 12 oz) rump steak, thinly
  sliced across the grain (see Notes)
100 g (3 1/2 oz) watercress, trimmed
4 eggs (optional)

1 To make the sauce, dissolve the dashi granules in 125 ml (1/2 cup) water in a bowl. Add the soy sauce, sake, mirin and caster sugar and stir until combined.

2 Drain the noodles, place in a large heatproof bowl, cover with boiling water and soak for 2 minutes. Rinse in cold water and drain well.

3 Melt the lard in a large frying pan over medium heat. Cook the spring onion, shiitake mushrooms and beef in batches, stirring continuously, for 1–2 minutes each batch, or until just brown. Return all the meat, spring onion and shiitake to the pan, then add the sauce and watercress. Cook for 1 minute, or until heated through and the watercress has wilted— the sauce needs to just cover the ingredients but not drown them.

4 To serve, divide the noodles among four serving bowls and spoon the sauce evenly over the top. If desired, crack an egg into each bowl and break up through the soup using chopsticks until it partially cooks.

NUTRITION PER SERVE
Fat 27.5 g; Protein 54 g; Carbohydrate 46 g; Dietary Fibre 5 g; Cholesterol 342 mg; 2755 kJ (660 Cal)

COOK'S FILE
Notes: Shirataki noodles are a jelly-like noodle, made from the starch of the devil's tongue plant. They are often packed in water, in clear sausage-shaped plastic packets, sold in the refrigerated section in Japanese supermarkets. They are also sold in cans, but the quality is not as good. To help you cut the meat into very thin slices, wrap the beef in plastic wrap and freeze for 40 minutes, or until partially frozen.

Sukiyaki is traditionally cooked on a portable gas ring in the centre of a table, as the guests cook their own portions. Each guest has a small bowl into which they crack a fresh egg. The hot contents of the wok are dipped into the egg before they are eaten.

Rinse the noodles well in a colander, under cold running water.

Cook the hotpot briefly until the watercress has just wilted.

CHICKEN WITH PONZU SAUCE AND SOMEN NOODLES

Preparation time: 15 minutes +
  overnight refrigeration
Cooking time: 45 minutes
Serves 4

Ponzu sauce
1 tablespoon lemon juice
1 tablespoon lime juice
1 tablespoon rice vinegar
1 tablespoon tamari
1 1/2 tablespoons mirin
2 1/2 tablespoons Japanese soy sauce
5 cm (2 inch) piece kombu (kelp),
  wiped with a damp cloth
1 tablespoon bonito flakes

900 g (2 lb) chicken thighs, trimmed
  and cut in half across the bone
10 cm (4 inch) piece kombu (kelp)

200 g (7 oz) dried somen noodles
250 g (9 oz) fresh shiitake mushrooms
  (cut into smaller pieces if too large)
1 carrot, thinly sliced
300 g (10 1/2 oz) baby English spinach
  leaves

1 To make the sauce, combine all the ingredients in a non-metallic bowl. Cover with plastic wrap and refrigerate overnight, then strain through a fine sieve.
2 Place the chicken and kombu in a large saucepan with 875 ml (3 1/2 cups) water. Bring to a simmer over medium heat and cook for 20 minutes, or until the chicken is cooked, skimming the scum off the surface. Remove the chicken pieces and strain the broth. Transfer the broth and chicken pieces to a 2.5 litre (10 cup) flameproof casserole dish or Japanese nabe. Cover the dish and

continue to cook over low heat for 15 minutes.
3 Meanwhile, cook the noodles in a large saucepan of boiling water for 2 minutes, or until tender. Drain and rinse under cold running water.
4 Add the mushrooms and carrot to the chicken and cook for 5 minutes. Place the noodles on top of the chicken, then top with the spinach. Cook, covered, for 2 minutes, or until the spinach has just wilted. Stir in 4–6 tablespoons of the ponzu sauce, or to taste. Serve immediately.

NUTRITION PER SERVE
Fat 9 g; Protein 32 g; Carbohydrate 37 g; Dietary Fibre 6.5 g; Cholesterol 98 mg; 1515 kJ (360 Cal)

COOK'S FILE
Note: Traditionally, this dish would be served in a ceramic nabe dish, for your guests to help themselves.

INDEX

This edition published in 2003 by Bay Books, an imprint of Murdoch Magazines Pty Limited,
GPO Box 1203, Sydney NSW 2001.

Editorial Director: Diana Hill
Editor: Stephanie Kistner
Creative Director: Marylouise Brammer
Designers: Michèle Chan, Vivien Valk
Food Director: Jane Lawson
Food Editors: Rebecca Clancy, Kathleen Gandy, Vanessa Broadfoot
Recipe Development: Alison Adams, Rekha Arnott, Vanessa Broadfoot, Rebecca Clancy,
Ross Dobson, Kathleen Gandy, Sonia Greig, Saskia Hay, Jane Lawson, Kate Murdoch,
Kim Passenger, John Skinner, Shauna Stockwell, Angela Tregonning
Home Economists: Alison Adams, Renèe Aiken, Sonia Greig, Kate Murdoch,
Kim Passenger, Angela Tregonning
Photographers: Ian Hofstetter, Craig Cranko
Food Stylists: Mary Harris, Carolyn Fienberg
Food Preparation: Ross Dobson, Kim Passenger
Nutritionist: Dr Susanna Holt

Chief Executive: Juliet Rogers
Publisher: Kay Scarlett

ISBN 1 74045 136 8.
Printed by Sing Cheong Printing Co. Ltd. PRINTED IN CHINA.

INTERNATIONAL GLOSSARY OF INGREDIENTS

capsicum · · · · · · · · · · red or green pepper	**spring onion** · · · · · · · · · scallion/shallot
chilli · · · · · · · · · · · chile, chili pepper	**telegraph cucumber** . long cucumber
coriander · · · · · · · · · · · cilantro	**tomato paste** (Aus.) · · tomato purée, double concentrate (UK)
eggplant · · · · · · · · · · aubergine	**tomato purée** (Aus.) · · sieved crushed tomatoes/passata (UK)
prawns · · · · · · · · · · · shrimp	**zucchini** · · · · · · · · · · courgette